by
David Arscott

with drawings by
David Marl

Pomegranate Press
Lewes, Sussex

For Rosie and Jack
who have all this to discover

Also by David Arscott in this Pomegranate Press series:
The Sussex Story - 'the most comprehensive Sussex history package ever devised'

Other Sussex books by the same author include:
Tales from the Parish Pump
The Upstart Gardener
Curiosities of East Sussex
Curiosities of West Sussex

with Warden Swinfen:
Hidden Sussex/People of Hidden Sussex/
Hidden Sussex Day by Day/Hidden Sussex - the Towns

Video narration:
Discovering Brighton
Discovering West Sussex

Cover photograph by David Arscott: *Ox-eye daisies in South Malling churchyard, Lewes*

Back cover illustrations. left to right: *jew's ear fungus on elder; fox; barn owl with prey; badger; gravestone colonised by vegetation, South Malling*

Printed by Flexiprint Ltd, Lancing, Sussex
Copyright © David Arscott
Published in 1994 by Pomegranate Press, Preston House, Lewes BN7 2NS

British Library Cataloguing-in-Publication Data.
A catalogue record for this book is available from the British Library

ISBN 0 9519876 1 5

*C*halk grassland and acid heath, oak woodland and grazing marsh, sea cliff and ghyll valley: we live among improbable riches. Not only is our Sussex landscape both varied and beautiful, but a lucky combination of geology, climate and relentless human exploitation has produced the conditions which, for ecologists, make this county one of the most interesting in Britain. Here we find plants and insects which properly belong in the warmth of continental Europe; others which are relics of a cooler, moister age many thousands of years ago.

Man's part in the endless processes of change and adaptation has been crucial. It was our prehistoric forbears, hacking clearings for their livestock, who inadvertently created the sandstone heaths we value today. Later generations ploughed fields, dug out ponds, planted hedgerows, dammed rivers, coppiced the woods of the Weald, covered the Downs with sheep, quarried for chalk and stone, built canals and roads and railways - and all the time, awaiting its chance, a teeming multitude followed close behind.

The making of the landscape and the resourcefulness of the wildlife which occupies it are the twin themes of this book. The ways of their perpetual interweaving are often surprising and occasionally baffling: anyone who sets out to explore the complex world of bird, beast and flower soon comes to realise that to walk only a few yards may be to traverse a dozen miniature universes, each with its own subtle interplay of warmth, light, moisture and trace minerals, each with its distinctive flora and fauna. In concentrating, as we must, on the major types of habitat, we should always remember that this area of beech wood or that stretch of river bank may be quite unlike another (and we may thereby find it possible to forgive an author who excites the expectation of meeting a particular bee or butterfly which obstinately refuses to materialise on cue). Nature is not packaged for our convenience, even in the many excellent reserves which feature in these pages.

Any popular guide must establish its own rules and limitations. I have used Latin names only where no others exist; have, for aesthetic reasons, generally avoided the use of capital letters save in the obvious places; and have ignored many of the strange hyphenations which festoon botanical names like so much choking bindweed. I have, moreover, concentrated unashamedly (although not exclusively) on those 'greatest hits' of the natural world - birds, butterflies and mammals, flowering plants and trees.

But these are trivialities. What matters above all is that we should understand the peculiar demands of our wildlife in order to preserve its dazzling diversity. This is an account, fragmentary though it may be, of how it was coping as the twentieth century evolved into the twenty-first.

David Arscott

ACKNOWLEDGEMENTS

A great many people have contributed to whatever success this book may have. Thanks, first, to David Lang, who looked over the authorial shoulder throughout, and to David Harvey (English Nature), Glynn Jones (West Sussex countryside manager, National Trust), David Streeter (pro vice-chancellor, University of Sussex) and Tony Whitbread (conservation officer, Sussex Wildlife Trust) who read the complete text before publication. This is not the work any of them would have written, and they are responsible for none of its deficiencies, but it would certainly have been much the poorer without their suggestions and corrections.

A grateful roll of honour can only hint at the range of expertise offered by those other naturalists, amateur and professional, who gave so generously of their time and knowledge: Jeremy Adams, John Cooper, Gerald Legg (Booth Museum of Natural History); Peter Bateman (director, Rentokil); Phil Belden (Brighton Urban Wildlife Group); Norman Day (Forestry Commission): Mike Edwards (bees and wasps); Peter Gay (Butterfly Conservation); Ann Griffiths (county ecologist, West Sussex); Paul Harmes (Sussex Botanical Recording Society; BSBI recorder for East Sussex); Colin Hedley (Farming and Wildlife Advisory Group); Reg Hinks (butterflies and ants); Peter Hodge (beetles); Tony Hutson (Bat Conservation Trust); Ed Jarzembowski (Brighton Borough Council); Tony Mouzer (Dutch elm disease); Roger Musselle (garden wildlife); John Newnham (Sussex Ornithological Society); Keith Noble (RSPB); Colin Palmer (Forestry Commission); Ben Perkins (walk routes); Colin Pratt (moths and butterflies); Phil Robertson (marine wildlife); Francis Rose (ancient woodland); David Saunders (trees and woodlands officer, East Sussex county council); Alex Tate (county ecologist, East Sussex); Graham Thompson (ranger, Hastings Country Park); Andy Tittensor (mammals); Alan Wheeler (bird migration); Richard Williamson (warden, Kingley Vale nature reserve); Barry Yates (warden, Rye Harbour nature reserve).

Photographs and other illustrative material were kindly supplied by: Booth Museum of Natural History (map, p5); Peter Bateman/Rentokil (pests 34, 35); Ben Darby (Kingley Vale yew 15, Devil's Dyke scrub 33, Pagham saltmarsh 49, Pevensey Levels 65, reedbeds 67); Doreen Darby (beech at Stanmer 61); Robert Eade (emerald damselfly 17, skylark young 20, banded demoiselle 39, marsh frog 65, banded agrion 71, fox, barn owl and badger *back cover);* David Harvey (mouse-eared bat 8, the Mens 11, Castle Hill sward 21, Seven Sisters 27, Lullington Heath 44 & 45, River Arun 71); Reg Hinks (video film of ants and caterpillars 74,75); John Holloway (felled beech 51, starlings over Royal Pavilion 57, furrowed farmland 82); David Lang (glow-worm 14, wayfaring tree berries 32, fly orchid, burnt orchid, Adrena bee & early spider orchid 46); Parham Park (antler trophies 80, deer 81); Tim Sharman (wallaby and deer 7, Ashdown Forest 16, Buchan Country Park 39); Graham Thompson (Dripping Well, fungi 23, sandstone cliffs, nesting fulmar 30); Tom Wright (High Beeches meadow 59).

Thanks, too, to Bob Armstrong, Loni von Grüner and Ann Varley for their much appreciated help.

CONTENTS   *page*

Introduction:

LORDS OF CREATION

Twenty million years ago a titanic collision between two vast land masses thrust their clashing and grinding edges thousands of feet into the air to form the great jagged mountain range of the Alps. It was that same epic event which, sending juddering ripples hundreds of miles in all directions, created the fractured landscape in which the wildlife of Sussex lives today. The solid earth rose, cracked and buckled. Where once there had been orderly layers of sands, clays and chalk, deposited over millenia in fresh and salt water and gradually hardened into rock, there was now a mighty dome with the oldest material forced up at its centre, the youngest peeled back to form its outer rim.

The relentless assault and battery of the elements over the intervening millions of years, crumbling the softer rocks and scouring out river valleys, has served to present the evidence of that colossal eruption with great clarity. The rim of our so-called 'Wealden anticline' is chalk, sweeping west from Beachy Head as the South Downs and turning through Hampshire to become the North Downs of Surrey and Kent. Within this chalk perimeter, in more or less orderly sequence, are bands of the rock which once lay beneath it. In Sussex we find, first, narrow strips of Upper Greensand and Gault Clay immediately north of the Downs; next a belt of Lower Greensand which, widening considerably in the west, forms considerable hills and, rising to 919ft at Black Down near the Surrey border, gives us the county's highest point; after this, the heavy, clinging clays of the Low Weald, once legendary for their impassability; and finally, running from Horsham down to the sea at Hastings, the jumble of very old sandstones and clays which form the forest ridges and deep ghyll valleys of the High Weald.

To visit the coast between Eastbourne and Hastings is to see the pattern laid out for convenient inspection. At Beachy Head, where the chalk cliffs meet the sea, the famous lighthouse sits on a ledge of Upper Greensand, while a band of Gault Clay can be seen a little further to the east. Beyond Eastbourne the clays of the Low Weald emerge at the coast as the Pevensey Levels. East again, the fossil-rich High Weald sandstone rears up as the honeycombed cliffs of Hastings and Fairlight. The one area which falls outside this geological formation is the western coastal fringe between Shoreham and Chichester, a swathe of fertile soils and gravel which was once covered by the sea.

Such diversity in so small an area accounts in part for the richness of our Sussex wildlife today. Most plants and animals are extremely fussy about the conditions in which they will thrive: the carpenter bee *Ceratina cyanea*, to give but one striking example, breeds only in dead bramble stems above short grassland. Specific demands such as these, evolved over countless generations, must

THE SURFACE GEOLOGY OF SUSSEX

Alluvium	Reading Beds	Lower Greensand	Wadhurst Clay
Brickearth	Woolwich Beds	Weald Clay	Ashdown Sand
Gravels	Chalk	Paludina limestone	Fairlight Clays
Clay-with-flints	Upper Greensand	Horsham Stone	Purbeck Beds
London Clay	Gault	Tunbridge Wells Sand	

The herbivorous iguanodon, about 12ft tall, left its footprints in the sands of Wealden river deltas. It was given its name by the surgeon and geologist Dr Gideon Mantell, whose house near Lewes Castle carries a commemorative plaque.

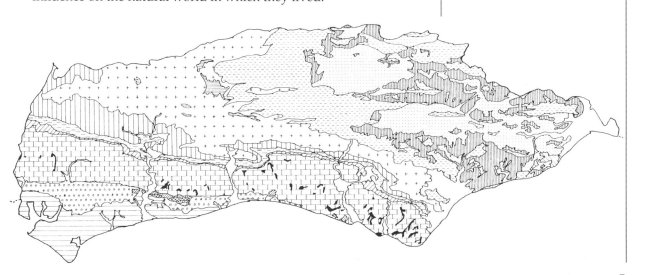

DR. GIDEON A. MANTELL F.R.S.
SURGEON AND GEOLOGIST
BORN IN LEWES 1790, DIED IN LONDON 1852
LIVED HERE
HE DISCOVERED THE FOSSIL BONES OF
THE PREHISTORIC IGUANODON
IN THE SUSSEX WEALD

necessarily contain their own built-in vulnerability, but the variety of wealden, downland and coastal habitats consequently supports an improbable profusion of living things.

A second major influence is the climate. Sussex, at the northernmost fringe of the European range, attracts some species which more properly belong in warmer areas across the Channel but which manage a somewhat precarious existence here. Many of our butterflies and orchids, for instance, are typically south European: with a cooling of the climate we would almost certainly lose them, whereas the onset of longer and hotter summers might well increase their numbers. Yet small shifts such as these are as nothing when compared with the swings of temperature experienced during the long prehistoric period when Britain was still a part of the Continental landmass. The first men and women in Sussex lived alongside sabre tooth tigers and elephants in a warm interglacial period when sea levels were about a hundred feet higher than today, after which the chill fingers of the last Ice Age were to beckon such exotica as the mammoth and the woolly rhinoceros. Later, as the ice cap slowly retreated, the area was home to the polar bear, the arctic fox, the musk ox and the reindeer.

Sussex became this island's southern frontier some eight thousand years ago, when the infiltrating sea at last sundered Britain from Europe. It was a densely wooded terrain, covered by trees such as oak and elm, lime, pine, hazel, birch and alder: the fossilised remains of a submerged prehistoric forest (gnarled oak and hazel trunks) can still be seen off Bexhill at very low tides. The inhabitants were hunter-gatherers, a nomadic people who fashioned flint knives and arrow-heads to attack their prey but who were not yet what they were very soon to become - the third great influence on the natural world in which they lived.

Places to visit

• *Dinosaur footprints:*
between Cooden
199: TQ 710063
and Pett Level
189: TQ 904145

• *Fossils:*
Covehurst Wood,
Hastings Country Park
199: TQ 850103

• *Submerged prehistoric forest:*
between Bexhill
199: TQ 760075
and Pett Level
189: TQ 905145

Prehistoric remains:

• *Booth Museum,*
Dyke Road, Brighton
(01273) 552586
198: TQ 301058

• *Bexhill Museum,*
Egerton Road
(01424) 211769
199: TQ 737072

(and see museums list in the companion volume, 'The Sussex Story', p 86)

4300 BC

Neolithic period. First farmers settle Sussex, felling and burning trees. Wild boar, brown bear, red deer, beaver, wolf, polecat, pine marten. Climate becomes drier. Abandoned clearings colonised by heather, birch and ash

1500 BC

Bronze Age. Increase of agriculture, cultivation and pasture at the expense of woodland. Spread of grassland for grazing animals: crop weeds such as cornflower and charlock become established. House mouse introduced

700BC

Iron Age. Stronger ploughs allow more extensive arable farming. Climate becomes cool and wet. Beech, birch, pine and yew increase. Lime extinct

43 AD

Roman invasion of Britain. Villas, urban settlements with gardens: Mediterranean vines, fruits, herbs and trees. Coastal plain becomes a granary

406AD

Roman legions withdraw from Britain. Intensified Saxon raids, followed by settlement. Saxon farmers gradually colonise the Weald

It was the first farmers who, wielding flint axes and lighting fires to create clearings in the forests for their crops and livestock, began that profound humanisation of the landscape which today seems to threaten its very survival. The analysis of ancient pollen from Iping Common, west of Midhurst, has revealed that hazel abruptly gave way to heather as the dominant ground cover around 4300BC, almost certainly because of shrub clearance and subsequent grazing by livestock. The gradual spread of grassland from about 4000BC at Lewes Brooks likewise suggests the pasturage of cattle and sheep on newly-colonised terrain. Not all of the early settlements were permanent, and fast-growing trees such as birch and ash were ready to take advantage of any abandoned areas, but by the end of the neolithic period there must already have been considerable swathes of cultivated ground in Sussex - a remarkably swift conquest of the wilderness which the steady improvement of ploughs and other implements was to accelerate in the centuries before the Romans arrived.

Introduced mammals: when they arrived in Sussex	
House mouse	neolithic
Fallow deer	late 11th century
Rabbit	12th century
Black rat	12th century
Brown rat	early 18th century
Yellow-necked mouse	19th century
Grey squirrel	19th century
Red-necked wallaby	20th century
North American mink	20th century
Chinese muntjac deer	20th century
Japanese sika deer	20th century

This is perhaps difficult to credit from our own disturbed, self-flagellating, rape-of-the-planet perspective, but the historical period begins with a landscape already substantially transformed by the activities of our predecessors. The denser areas of the Weald may have so far resisted penetration (the land-hungry Saxons were to be the great despoilers there), but the Romans found a region extensively farmed, its cultivated fields spreading not only over the fertile coastal plain and along the valley bottoms, but even across the unpromising slopes of the Downs (where they can still be traced today, shown as 'ancient field systems' on Ordnance Survey maps). To this thriving economy the new masters brought their characteristic order and control, building splendid villas at the centre of large wheat-growing estates (the one at Bignor being particularly luxurious) and exploiting the iron which they found in the forests of the Weald: the slag remains at many of their 'bloomery' sites.

But if urban development, agriculture and industry are now widely seen as rapacious enemies of the natural world, that is surely a reflection of the scale and efficiency of our own, comparatively recent, destructiveness. In the past, man's changing hand brought diversity rather than annihilation. Just as those first, slash-and-burn farmers created the tracts of sandy heathland and chalk grassland we value today, so most of the subsequent scarrings and reshapings of the landscape, however ugly some may be, have usefully increased the range of habitats available to wildlife: clay and gravel pits, houses and gardens, roadside verges, hedgerows, reservoirs. We should at least remember that heavy-handed *Homo sapiens* has, for all his faults, produced a much more varied landscape than the one he found. While about a fifth of our native woodland mammals have disappeared from Sussex, with creatures such as the beaver, wolf and wild boar long since hunted to extinction, many of the plants and animals in our soiled Eden would not be here without us.

Sometimes we can point to deliberate gains rather than lucky spin-offs. Neolithic farmers (who also, inadvertently, seem first to have played host to the house mouse), brought in cattle, sheep and other domestic animals. The Romans sought to maintain some of the luxuries they were accustomed to at home by importing to Sussex a wide range of herbs, vegetables and fruit trees - the recreated formal garden at Fishbourne is planted with many of them. The Normans introduced fallow deer as a reliable source of meat throughout the long winter months and

Two that got away. The red-necked wallaby is an unlikely feature of the Sussex mammals list, a small colony having survived in the High Weald area since escaping from a menagerie at Leonardslee in the 1940s. The grazing fallow deer in the background are likewise descendants of introduced stock which absconded.

constructed extensive warrens where they bred rabbits for the pot.

These last two species point up a general rule: if conditions in the wild are to their liking, captive breeds will eventually escape and multiply. This accounts for the unlikely presence on Sussex wildlife lists of the Indian ring-necked parakeet (to see a flock screeching overhead in the Hollingbury area of Brighton is an uncanny experience) and the bounding red-necked wallaby, a native of New South Wales. The brown rat, the grey squirrel, the North American mink and the marsh frog are instructive examples of the swiftness with which incomers can seize an opportunity and show similar native species how to dominate a territory. Plants can be successful absconders, too, and some of the beautiful rhododendrons which have adapted so well to the acid soils of famous High Weald gardens such as Leonardslee and Wakehurst Place have in many places spread beyond their stately enclosures to become veritable weeds. Two particularly unwelcome escapees have been Japanese knot-weed (introduced as a garden plant by the Victorians, but now out of control in the wild, where its spreading roots will break up tarmac and concrete), and giant hogweed, which grows to all of twelve feet and is liable to give anyone who touches it a nasty rash.

Naturalised exotica. The striking common pheasant, first brought to England before the Norman conquest, has bred in the wild for centuries and is today a familiar motoring hazard, but the equally showy rhododendrons (extensively planted for game cover in the nineteenth century) have also escaped their confines. The purple flowered Rhododendron ponticum *from Asia Minor is the most successful runaway, forming dense thickets which often shade out other plants.*

• Bronze Age farm & fields:
New Barn Down, Patching
197: TQ 084093

Other ancient field systems:

• Chantry Hill
197: TQ 080118
• Thundersbarrow Hill
198: TQ 230084
• Balmer Down
198: TQ 365111
• Malling Hill
198: TQ 425108
• Windover Hill
199:TQ 545035
• Jevington
199: TQ 568031

• Bignor Roman Villa
(017987) 259
197: SU 987147

• Fishbourne Roman Palace
(01243) 785859
197: SU 840052

(for other early examples of man's impact on the landscape - including neolithic flint mines, Iron Age hill-forts and Roman bloomery sites - see margins of 'The Sussex Story')

1066
Norman Conquest. Royal hunting forests and deer parks

12th-13th centuries
Large-scale reclamation of coastal marshes. Wealden oaks provide top-quality timber for ship-building industry

1349
Black rat brings the Plague to Sussex. Sharp decline in population; deserted villages; agricultural decay

16th-17th centuries
Wealden iron masters and glass blowers consume vast quantities of timber: hammerponds created. Widespread enclosures of common land

1693
Royal Commission decree on enclosure of Ashdown Forest grants commoners 6,400 acres for grazing

late 18th/early 19th century
Period of agricultural improvements. High corn prices during Napoleonic wars lead to extensive ploughing of the Downs, where there are also huge flocks of sheep. Canals and turnpike roads link corn-growing Sussex to London market. Wealthy landowners develop large landscaped parks

19th century
From 1840, railways dissect Sussex countryside, encouraging growth of new commuter settlements

20th century
Countryside increasingly threatened by urban sprawl; road building; coastal development; intensive farming with artificial chemicals

So how abundant is our Sussex wildlife today? The basic statistics can hardly fail to astonish the layman conscious of only the few, most obvious kinds of bird, beast and flower. There are, for instance, more than 2,800 different beetles recorded from the county and probably a similar number of flies; five hundred lichens and a comparable tally of mosses and liverworts; more than three hundred bees and wasps; something like five hundred species of spider; and six hundred of the larger moths.

Even more startling, perhaps, are the wildlife counts at individual sites: the 400 species of fungi at Ebernoe Common (Sussex has arguably the richest fungus flora in Britain); the sixty types of seaweed at East Head, West Wittering; the three hundred moths in St Leonards Forest; and the count of more than a hundred lichens in the churchyard at Stopham. At Rye Harbour nature reserve upwards of 1850 invertebrates have been recorded, including 677 types of beetle, 439 butterflies and moths, 281 flies, 126 spiders and harvestmen, 87 ants, bees and wasps, 103 bugs and sixty species of slug and snail.

And yet, while an optimistic account would stress that Sussex remains the most wooded of English counties and would note, for good measure, such ecologically important areas as Ashdown Forest (accounting for seven per cent of Britain's lowland heath) and Chichester Harbour (where ten per cent of the world's dark-bellied brent geese regularly overwinter), there is no shortage of evidence to support a far gloomier view. The habitats available to wildlife may be as varied as ever, but many of them are shrinking ominously, and although introduced species such as the collared dove and little owl have spread rapidly in recent years, these are more than offset by those that have disappeared.

While the spread of bricks and concrete is one cause, our own blind efficiency is another: it was pump drainage rather than property development which sucked the wetlands dry, just as it was the introduction of powerful fertilisers and herbicides which

Missing, presumed dead. The last mouse-eared bat in Britain, not seen at its Sussex roost since 1990.

Vanished mammals: when they died out

ENGLAND		SUSSEX	
Lynx	neolithic	Red deer	early 19th century
Reindeer	neolithic	Wild cat	1850
Wild ox	neolithic	Polecat	1920s
Beaver	10th century	Pine marten	1920s
Brown bear	10th century	Black rat	1950s
Wolf	late 15th century	Red squirrel	1950s
Wild boar	late 17th century	Mouse-eared bat	1990s

made the ploughing of downland so profitable. If we find it comforting to blame this kind of damage on 'them', however, it is as well to realise that our own unremarkable activities can threaten sensitive areas, too. At the National Trust's Sullington Warren reserve, to give a graphic example, the perpetual exercising of dogs is transforming precious heath into tussocky grassland as their steadily accumulating droppings seep into the soil and enrich it.

A Sussex exclusive. The spiked rampion, seen here on a verge near Blackboys, is found nowhere in Britain but an area of East Sussex between Hadlow Down and Abbots Wood.

Today we find many species clinging to a precarious life in what, for them, are small oases in a large desert: otters, occasionally spotted in the clean waters of a West Sussex river but very close to extinction; orchids so rare that it would be folly to reveal their location; the remarkable lily-of-the-valley beds in a St Leonard's Forest nature reserve; the red star thistle (its seeds perhaps originally carried to England by soldiers returning from the Napoleonic wars) now surviving at only a few sites in Britain, including the Seven Sisters Country Park.

While most of our wildlife losses are attributable to disappearing habitats, others have a more direct cause. Peregrine falcons had colonised the chalk cliffs of Sussex for thousands of years, but the build up of powerful insecticides through the food chain made their eggs infertile and they stopped breeding after 1957. Buzzards, exterminated in Sussex during the 19th century, reestablished themselves in a small way in about 1950 but had disappeared again by 1976 - probably because of shooting by gamekeepers, although the sharp reduction in the rabbit population cause by myxomatotis may have been a contributory factor. The deliberate introduction of that foul disease in the 1950s not only wiped out some 99 per cent of the county's rabbits, but had the effect of sharply reducing the numbers of its chief predator, the stoat, at the same time allowing grass to sprout where once it had been nibbled short, with an inevitable smothering of the small flowers which grow in downland turf and the consequent decline in the populations of those butterflies which feed on them. Nothing lives, or dies, in isolation.

Some of the damage can be reversed if we care enough about it. Although the proverbial fecundity of rabbits has been sufficient to make them a menace to farmers once again, it was the banning of the most pernicious poisons which brought the buzzard back as a breeding species in the late 1980s and the peregrine in the 1990s. Similarly with the landscape: since nature, left to its own devices, would eventually clothe most of Sussex in dense woodland, the retention of a wide range of habitats demands our deliberate management.

We, in short, are the Lords of Creation now. We should doubtless accept the title with shame (because of our poor stewardship of the planet) and with humility (for storm and flood regularly reveal our limitations), but to deny responsibility for the world we share will be to proclaim its ultimate decay.

• *Trotton church*
197: SU 836225

some other churchyards with rare lichens, ferns, mosses and liverworts:

• *West Hoathly*
187: TQ 363326

• *Hartfield*
188: TQ 479357

• *Wadhurst*
188: TQ 641319

• *Sutton*
197: SU 979155

• *Slindon*
197: SU 961084

• *South Harting*
197: SU 784195

• *Stopham*
197: TQ 026189

• *Fittleworth*
197: TQ 009193

• *Pulborough*
197: TQ 047188

• *Shipley*
198: TQ 145218

• *Lily beds,*
St Leonards Forest
(Sussex Wildlife Trust)
187: TQ 212308

Oak

Rowan

Redstart

Wood Sanicle

Wood Mouse

IN THE WILDWOOD

To plunge into the dense woodland of The Mens, between Billingshurst and Petworth, is to hear the echo of ancestral voices. The tracks and banks you stumble upon are too ancient to date with any precision, and the occasional open areas between the giant oaks and beeches are the remnants of 'assarts' - forest clearings illicitly hacked in medieval times. The glory of this landscape, however, is what has not been touched. No area of Sussex has escaped man's shaping hand, but The Mens was a woodland common for a thousand years and then lay neglected for another hundred: it is, in part at least, as close to its virgin state as any you will find in the south of England.

An unchecked cycle of decay and regeneration gave the original Sussex wildwood an enormous diversity of growing things. A fifth of its trees would be dead at any one time, their decomposition returning nutrients to a fertile acid soil. While the gaps they left were randomly colonised by successive layers of seedlings, bushes, shrubs and saplings, the grazing of large animals – bears, red deer, wild cattle – helped keep open a scattering of sun-dappled glades. In an area the size of The Mens (about 380 acres) we might expect some forty kinds of shrubs and trees and at least 400 species of fungi, 300 flowering herbs and ferns, a hundred lichens, a hundred mosses and liverworts.

The Mens today reveals its kinship with this early deciduous wildwood, not least in that astonishing variety. In some places the oaks and beeches are tall and narrow-crowned, having stretched towards the light over hundreds of years in dense forest conditions. Elsewhere, by contrast, the trees spread their crowns, evidence of more open surroundings. Where they are dying, a great host of insects and fungi has swarmed to the feast. The invading shrubs include rowan, spindle and midland hawthorn.

Tracts of what botanists term ancient semi-natural woodland can be found throughout Sussex, and those irregular strips known as 'shaws' which are a feature of the High Weald landscape are believed to be remnants of the old wildwood. One good indicator is the presence of the wild service tree, which survives today only in venerable oak and ash woods. The Mens has it, as does Ebernoe Common, an area which has probably been wooded since the last ice age and which was used by commoners over hundreds of years (indeed, into the early twentieth century) for grazing their livestock: holly scrub now flourishes beneath the trees where this so-called 'wood pasture' was practised. More than 300 species of plants and 400 of fungi have been counted at Ebernoe, where prized inhabitants include roe deer and the secretive woodcock in the depths of the woods, nightingales in the thickets.

Is there, then, a typical mature Sussex woodland? It may exist only in the mind, but we would surely expect a good sprinkling of oak, ash and thorn. The forest floor will be carpeted with wood anemones, violets, wood sanicle, butcher's broom, sweet woodruff and the tiny green flowers of that strange plant moschatel, otherwise known as town hall clock. We shall no doubt hope to see a fluttering of brimstone butterflies, speckled woods and silver-washed fritillaries, with a purple hairstreak - and, if we are really lucky, even a purple emperor - among the oaks. Is that a day-flying longhorn beetle we see feeding on the hawthorn blossom? Nearby, grey squirrels swiftly shin up a tree close to a badger sett by which our nostrils pick up the rank and unmistakable stench of fox. And there are deer, which have been steadily increasing their Sussex populations and from which we have a choice of fallow, roe, muntjac and sika.

Birds abound, of course: the three British woodpeckers (greater spotted, lesser spotted and green); a nuthatch and a tree creeper picking insects from the crevices in the bark; a pretty chorus of summer warblers; a jay which dashes into the trees, giving a glimpse of its bright blue wing-feathers and a flash of its vivid white rump; a breeding sparrowhawk; and (just possibly, for they are becoming scarcer) a pair of redstarts along the woodland edges. When darkness falls and woodmice forage in the litter of the forest floor, bats will flit above our heads and we shall hear the fierce *kee-wick* of a tawny owl.

To see some species we shall have to visit a few specific locations. Dormice, for instance, occur only at scattered sites in East and West Sussex. Hornets, relatively rare in the county, regularly nest in hollow trees at Kingspark Wood, Plaistow. And the rare beard lichen, which looks like strings of tiny white sausages, is known only in Eastdean Park and West Dean Woods, where it grows high up on the trees.

The Mens, near Pulborough. The ancient Sussex woodlands offered wildlife a rich variety of habitats, with sunlit open glades among dense stands of trees.

Oyster Catchers

Spear Thistle

Horned Poppy

Seakale

Shelduck

OF TIME AND TIDES

*T*he capricious sea has mocked a good many human endeavours, and its regular harvest of drifting sand and pebbles, carried eastwards along the Sussex beaches and hurled ashore by great storms, offers one of nature's sharper reminders of our fragility. A great shingle spit (today's Shoreham Beach) accumulated at the mouth of the Adur during the middle ages, cutting the great port of Shoreham from the sea and carrying the river some three miles to the east before an artificial cut was made. The Ouse, which appears to have met the sea close to its present outlet in Roman times, was in similar fashion gradually diverted to Seaford until yet further deposits choked that important medieval port and a man-made cut created a 'new haven' back to the west.

In the far west, the shingle spits across the mouth of Pagham Harbour have shifted endlessly and dramatically, and the entrance is today kept open by steel retaining walls. In the east, the Rother is another river to have changed its course. Camber Castle was an impregnable state-of-the-art fortress when Henry VIII built it on the rim of Rye Bay in 1539, but it looks very much like a folly today: successive shingle banks have stranded it all of a mile inland. The martello tower of 1807, erected at the harbour mouth as a deterrent to Napoleon, likewise squats far from the lapping waves.

However chastening this may be to those of a philosophical turn of mind, the fact is that the undulating grassland around Camber Castle (part of it within Rye Harbour nature reserve) now serves as an invaluable botanical clock. Records of the major storms which threw up these substantial ridges allow changes in the coastline to be traced over hundreds of years, thus enabling ecologists to gauge the rate at which plants colonise the ridges as they build up ever more fertile concentrations of litter and humus. There are, moreover, a great many specialised plants in these older areas, together with some rare bees and beetles - although the amateur naturalist is unlikely to thrill to the knowledge that the weevil *Limobius mixtus* (which has, to prove the point, no popular name) is found nowhere in Britain but here.

What seems much more remarkable is the ability of a wide range of plants to live on apparently bare shingle constantly blown by keen, salt-laden winds. Indeed, the sheer improbability of such a thing must leave this habitat vulnerable to destruction, and there have been significant losses to quarrying and housing development at the Crumbles, east of Langney Point, and at Shoreham Beach. But this landscape is *not* dead. During the winter months the vegetation can look very sorry for itself, but in late May and June the beach at Rye Harbour is bright with the blooms of sea kale, sea pea and the yellow horned poppy.

Succulent leaves and long taproots are common adaptations to the drying effects of salt and wind: sea kale, for example, copes with the hostile conditions by putting down long, anchoring roots as much as three feet into the pebbles where humus has accumulated and where fresh water lingers. Good dispersal is essential on shingle, too. The kale's numerous rounded seed pods (a tasty meal for wood mice, as well as for large flocks of greenfinches which have beaks stout enough to crack them open) are washed along the shore on the tide, whereas spear thistle and ragwort have their seeds carried away by the wind.

While both Rye and Pagham harbours are noted for their rich shingle vegetation (Pagham's includes the only British colony of the June-flowering childing pink), most visitors are attracted to them by the prodigious influx of birds which flock to their open water. Summer may be the quietest period for ornithologists (winter sees the mass arrival of refugees from the frozen arctic, and the spring and autumn months are abuzz with passing migrants), but this is when oystercatchers, shelduck, redshank and lapwing come to breed - and it is now that the shingle banks become a vital habitat for ringed plovers and, most important of all, for the ground-nesting terns.

At Rye, where common, little and sandwich terns have bred successfully, electric fencing has been erected against foxes and a team of 80 volunteers keeps a vigil over the sensitive areas. At Pagham, where wardens also patrol, the Church Norton shingle spit is fenced off from the public each summer to prevent disturbance of the little terns.

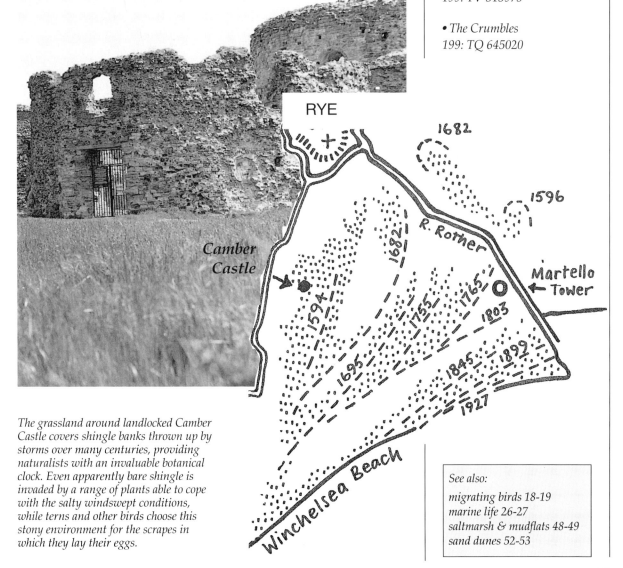

The grassland around landlocked Camber Castle covers shingle banks thrown up by storms over many centuries, providing naturalists with an invaluable botanical clock. Even apparently bare shingle is invaded by a range of plants able to cope with the salty windswept conditions, while terns and other birds choose this stony environment for the scrapes in which they lay their eggs.

Red wing

Yew

Mistle

thrush

THE GREAT YEW FOREST

*I*n the September of 1963 Richard Williamson motorcycled down to Sussex and discovered, on the steep slopes of a dry chalk coombe, a 'sinister and fantastic' forest which had raised the neck hairs and touched the imagination of a clutch of Victorian writers. The son of *Tarka the Otter* author Henry Williamson, he would himself later write a vivid account of his experiences as warden of Kingley Vale and its ancient, twisted yews - the finest natural grove anywhere in Europe.

'It was to be a year or two before I came to terms with that enclosing canopy of trees that stretched for nearly a mile,' he confessed in *The Great Yew Forest*, describing a dark interior where no plants grew and where the waxy red fruit of the female trees, glimmering like Chinese lanterns, provided a twilight autumn feast for migrating flocks of mistle and song thrushes, blackbirds, fieldfares and

Glow-worm on dwarf thistle. Beyond the yews, Kingley Vale has large areas of old chalk grassland.

redwings. 'In several small and subtle ways its character was not always benign; it did not yield easily to a mind used to birds and open skies, the more obvious side of nature. It would be no exaggeration to say that at times it was hostile.'

There is good chalk grassland and scrub at Kingley Vale, and even a patch of rare chalk heath, but it is the yews which especially fascinate and amaze. Those groping, spiralling branches are indeed the stuff of an eerie Germanic folktale. That dim interior under the dense foliage surely is a haunted place: on a hot summer day the temperature will be a full ten degrees lower than the sun-warmed chalk turf outside. And the leaves, bark and seeds (though not the red 'arils' of those bright berries) are notoriously toxic: bullocks, heifers and horses have all been killed after feasting at Kingley Vale.

How old are these wide-spreading giants? The yew is certainly our longest-living tree. Sacred in most European mythologies, its evergreen foliage a metaphor for immortality, it has been planted in burial grounds from pagan times, and a famous few have taken advantage of favourable and protected positions in our churchyards to reach an incredible age: the huge hollowed-out specimen at Crowhurst in East Sussex may well be a thousand years old. None of those at Kingley Vale is able to match such a prodigious longevity, but the oldest may already have been saplings in 1483 when Richard III ordered a general planting of yew to supply the makers of the deadly English longbow.

Although the largest here has a circumference of more than twenty feet, however, girth alone is no safe guide. For one thing, the yew's habit of fusing with a neighbouring tree can easily mislead the unwary; for another, a frail-looking tree with a mere two-inch circumference will often prove to be of exactly the same age as its hefty five-foot neighbour - perhaps all of a hundred years.

Regeneration is not easy for these yews. The seeds, assuming that they survive the predations of hungry mice, require frosty conditions in the early stages to break down the seedcase, followed by warm spring weather which will allow them to sprout. Germination can be delayed by up to three years, and in most cases the embryo tree still comes to nothing. The emerging saplings need the protection of shrubs in the early stages, but this vital cover has been steadily reduced by grazing rabbits and hares, and most seriously by growing populations of roe and fallow deer - all of which are able to browse on yew itself without harm.

Many of the yews started life under a protective spread of juniper, another native species which is much less common than it used to be and, in Sussex, is now confined to downland. Williamson discovered a veritable forest of dead junipers under the yews, their trunks polished by the claws of climbing mice: 'Most of them had never had a chance when their precocious foster-children, one year under their skirts, the next at their shoulder, the next trying to hold hands over the heads of their nursemaids, had started to grow. The juniper skeletons were of the round, short, well-branched structure which they had developed against the attacks of what they thought were their only enemies, the sheep, the deer and the wind; but in the event death had come from within the ranks.'

One of the oldest trees at Kingley Vale, the finest yew forest in Europe. Victorian writers found its dark interior 'sinister and fantastic'.

• *Kingley Vale*
(English Nature)
197: SU 826100

other yew woods:

• *West Harting Down*
197: SU 760175

• *North Marden Down*
197: SU 800168

ancient churchyard yews:

• *Stedham*
197: SU 864226

• *Coldwaltham*
197: TQ 023166

• *Buxted*
199: TQ 499236

• *Wilmington*
199: TQ 544043

• *Crowhurst*
199: TQ 758124

see also:

chalk grassland 20-21
chalk scrub 32-33
chalk heath 44-45

Scots Pine

Cotton Grass

Silver-Studded Blue

Bracken

JOHN OF GAUNT'S HUNTING GROUND

No tract of land in Sussex has been more ruthlessly exploited and acrimoniously fought over than Ashdown Forest. Great lords owned it and industrialists ransacked it, but the obstinate commoners continued to insist on their ancient rights – and it is the ordinary man and woman who have won in the end. Today we all have access to the finest belt of heathland in the south east of England.

'Where are the trees?' newcomers will often ask. There *are* wooded areas, of course, but this was a forest in the Norman sense: a vast hunting chase which was enclosed, some time before the end of the thirteenth century, by a fenced bank which prevented the red and fallow deer from escaping. John of Gaunt, who held the forest from 1372 to 1399, was one of its most ardent huntsmen.

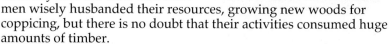

The hacking and burning of its trees had begun in prehistoric times and was to reach fever pitch during the sixteenth and seventeenth centuries when Wealden ironmasters enriched themselves by extracting ore from the local rock. Archaeologists currently take the view that these men wisely husbanded their resources, growing new woods for coppicing, but there is no doubt that their activities consumed huge amounts of timber.

As for the commoners, they played their own vital part in shaping the landscape we know, grazing their cattle on the forest, cutting bracken for their bedding and felling birch trees for firewood or repairs to their hovels. During the seventeenth century, new owners attempted to drive them out, but they tore down the fences of these would-be enclosers and won a famous victory when, in 1693, a Royal Commission awarded them 6,400 acres - the very area which is open to the public today.

The lack of trees over the greater part of Ashdown Forest is, in short, a blessing. It was continuous cutting and grazing, after all, which first produced these light, sandy, acid soils with their distinctive array of plants and insects. Scots pine and silver birch are nothing but vigorous weeds in this environment, and the rampaging bracken is a curse: now that the commoners no longer follow their traditional pursuits, teams of volunteers have to do the work of clearing the ground.

There are two distinct categories of heathland (and both can be seen at the Old Lodge reserve off the B2026). While stonechats, nightjars and the rare Dartford warbler are attracted to dry heath - areas of predominantly ling heather and gorse which swarm with insect life - naturalists prize the forest's wet heath even more because of its increasing scarcity.

This delicate environment is home to a number of specialised plants: the glorious marsh gentian, with its bright blue flowers in late summer; pink cross-leaved heath with its grey-green leaves;

purple moor grass, with its colonies of bog bush cricket; the fluffy white seed-heads of cotton grass; bog asphodel, massed with golden flowers during June and bearing orange seed pods throughout the autumn; sphagnum moss, able to hold twenty times its own weight of water; and sundews, which entice insects into their trap and then digest them.

Emerald damselfly on heather.

These boggy conditions, at Ashdown Forest and elsewhere, are a haunt of dragonflies: at Stedham Common alone no fewer than eleven species have been recorded. They also suit plants more usually associated with the north and west of Britain, such as marsh cinquefoil and the white-flowered bog bean. Both of these, together with marsh violet and cranberry, can be seen at the 'Black Hole' on Welch's Common, (part of the Burton Pond Nature Trail, south of Petworth), where moisture-loving trees such as alder, downy birch and sallow flourish on 15 acres of quaking peat. The visitors' leaflet points out that the boardwalk which gives a good view of the bog is used as a highway in the summer by wood ants, each of whose large, domed nests can contain a population of half a million.

Gorse thrives on the poor, acid soils of our heathlands, as here at Chailey Common. The rare Dartford warbler, which breeds in Sussex most years in very small numbers, builds its nest among the spiny branches.

Ashdown Forest
OS maps 187, 188, 198

• *Visitor centre, Wych Cross*
(01342) 3583
187: TQ 433324

• *Old Lodge nature reserve*
(Sussex Wildlife Trust)
188: TQ 469306

Ashdown Forest bogs at:
187: TQ 402328; 423306;
*   434326*
188: TQ 457323
188/198: TQ 453280

other bogs:
• *Heyshott Common*
197: SU 901193
• *Ambersham Common*
197: SU 913194
• *Welch's Common*
(West Sussex County
Council/
Sussex Wildlife Trust)
197: SU 980175
• *Hesworth Common*
(Fittleworth parish council)
197: TQ 004190
• *Bog Common*
197: TQ 067156

other wet acid heath:
• *Midhurst Common*
197: SU 873206
• *Lavington Common*
(National Trust)
197: SU 950190
• *Iping & Stedham Common*
(part Sussex Wildlife Trust)
197: SU 856218
• *Sullington Warren*
(National Trust)
198: TQ 096144
• *Chailey Common*
198: TQ 390215
• *Ditchling Common*
198: TQ 335180
• *Firehills*
(Hastings Country Park)
199: TQ 865112

OCEAN VAGABONDS

wheatears

Swallows

Terns

Bats do it, ladybirds do it, even flimsy butterflies and moths do it - but when it comes to following their wandering star, birds are in a class of their own. If spring and autumn are the most excitingly turbulent times, a restless pursuit of warmth, food and a mate ensures that never a month passes without some movement in our Sussex skies. Nearly every species migrates to a greater or lesser extent, the woodpeckers being so unadventurous an exception that they have yet to reach Ireland: even the 'resident' robin you see in the garden at Christmas may, in fact, be one of his Scandinavian cousins, your summer friend having slipped quietly south.

Seabirds which have been wintering in the sea around Africa begin to arrive here in March, but it is in April that the great biological rush to the breeding grounds brings the first major influx of birds to Sussex, with the arrival of whitethroats, blackcaps, redstarts, spotted flycatchers, house martins and swallows. The metronomic call of the chiffchaff and, a little later, the sweetly falling cadences of the willow warbler's song, precede the cuckoo as a harbinger of spring in our woodlands, while the downland turf will be graced by flocks of wheatears, flashing the brilliant white rumps which gave them their true countryman's name of 'white arse'. (These birds were regarded as such a delicacy for the table in former times that shepherds made a good income from trapping them, and they were so abundant that a single shepherd is on record as having caught 90 dozen in a day above Eastbourne). This is when the terns can be seen coming back from Africa, often harried along the coast by aggressive skuas which force them to release their catches of fish.

Any map of migration routes necessarily has to be a simplification. For some of these birds Sussex is the first landfall after a Channel crossing, but others hit the English coast further west and 'headland hop' to the east. Many will stay here to breed,

**BIRD MIGRATION
THROUGH SUSSEX**

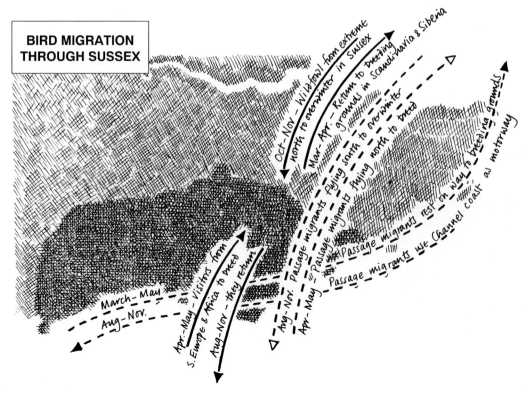

but still more are touching down for food and rest on their way further north and east. Inland waters are also useful for these passage migrants, and hungry ospreys will make occasional fishing expeditions over our reservoirs.

The ideal spring weather for ornithologists (though not for the birds themselves) is an area of high pressure over the Continent with a belt of rain along the Sussex coast: in these circumstances vast numbers of migrants will seek the nearest landfall, including rarities which had fully intended to give Sussex a miss. Similarly, an abrupt swing of the prevailing south-westerly wind to the south-east during a depression will bring passing seabirds down on our headlands. Large numbers of these birds are otherwise never even seen, although radar has tracked their passing high in the night sky.

The autumn return to warmer climes is a less urgent affair, beginning as early as July for some species but delayed until October or November for others. While the coast is again an ideal place to witness these movements, the chalk scrub valleys are busy with whitethroats, blackcaps and other warblers feasting on berries to fuel their impressively long flight south. This ability to find their way so accurately over thousands of miles remains something of a mystery. Some young birds fly in family flocks, but consider the achievement of a cuckoo: born in an alien nest, it will never have known its parents, yet it sets off from Sussex for Africa and – assuming that it avoids being shot down by those trigger-happy south European marksmen who enjoy blowing out of the sky anything that moves - will somehow return here unerringly the following spring.

Breeding may have finished, but the autumn sees the first arrivals of those birds which, escaping the frozen conditions of northern and central Europe, will spend the winter months around our Sussex river estuaries, marshes, reservoirs and gravel pits, where (thanks to the warming effect of the Gulf Stream) food and water are always available. This winter refuge is vital to the survival of brent and white-fronted geese, Bewick swans, waders such as grey plover, godwit and dunlin, and various species of duck. When an anticyclone stalls over Scandinavia, moreover, they will be joined by thousands more wildfowl desperately escaping the big freeze-up along the Baltic and North Sea coasts.

Harriers and short-eared owls are among the birds of prey which take shelter from the winter cold in Sussex, while flocks of redwings and fieldfares are regular visitors to our fields, parks and larger gardens.

Cuckoo

Barnacle geese

see also:

chalk scrub 32-33
saltmarsh 48-49
wetlands 64-65

Skylark

Round-headed Rampion

Marbled White

Yellow Rattle

A WALK IN PARADISE

*I*n the years around 1800 as many as 200,000 sheep grazed the chalk hills between Steyning and Eastbourne. It was these vast flocks which created the flower-sprinkled turf which we associate with the South Downs today. Although there are fine stands of shallow-rooting beeches on patches of the soil known as 'clay-with-flints', much of this landscape is bare of trees, especially at the eastern end of the range. Once upon a time, however, it was almost completely wooded: deep, fertile, acid soils have been found beneath the prehistoric burial mounds which rise like enormous grassy molehills all along the ridge. In preserving the Downs as we would like them to be we are, as so often in conservation, making a choice between different moments in time.

Hungry young skylarks in their downland nest.

What we wish to keep here is as unquestionably precious as it is threatened - a lovely landscape of scudding cloud-shadows over gentle green slopes where skylarks rise from a springy turf studded with violets, cowslips, harebells, orchids and a host of sweet-scented herbs (wild basil and marjoram and Kipling's 'close-bit thyme that smells/Like dawn in Paradise'), while little blue butterflies flit among the vetches. The territory of the brown hare and the rabbit, this is among the richest habitats in western Europe. The dry, dense sward, alive with bees and grasshoppers, glow-worms and chalk-loving snails, supports rare or localised plants such as 'the pride of Sussex', the round-headed rampion.

This is, we should be aware, a divided landscape, and to walk along the ridge is to pass between two habitats. The steeper, north-facing slopes, seeing less of the sun, are consequently cooler and damper than those which fall more gently southwards to the sea. The increasingly scarce Adonis blue butterfly is one species that will breed only on the southern faces of the Downs, since the temperatures on the far side are too low for its eggs to hatch. The marbled white and the dark green fritillary, by contrast, prefer the wetter northern region, its long, coarse grassland also being a haunt of the corn bunting, that 'fat bird of the barley'.

The thin rendzina soil of the old chalk grassland - rich in calcium but low in important plant nutrients such as nitrates, phosphates and iron, which sink almost without trace into the porous chalk - is a model demonstration ground for Darwin's 'survival of the fittest' theory. The fittest in this case are chiefly small, slow-growing plants which individually take little space, although in some areas there will be as many as forty species in one square yard of turf. The downland plants have different strategies for survival: thistles and plantains crudely elbow their rivals aside, whereas the likes of thyme and the beautiful bird's foot trefoil take a safety-in-numbers approach and grow in colonies. Remarkably, too, they have an ally in yellow rattle, a part-parasite which actually checks the growth of invading grasses by taking nourishment from their roots.

While the chalk grassland is obviously threatened by tree-planting, ploughing and the spraying of fertilisers (which give fast-growing, all-smothering plants their head), the farmer's neglect can prove just as damaging. In the absence of sheep, which severely declined in numbers after the first world war, only rabbits can be relied upon to keep the turf chewed short, and although their populations have almost recovered from the wretched myxomatosis outbreak of the 1950s, there will never be enough of them to do the job. Their uncontrolled, selective grazing can, in any case, prove damaging to some plant communities. If the land is left to itself, vigorous grasses such as cocksfoot and upright brome will soon swagger above the creeping herbs, to be followed in turn by tougher types still - woody shrubs which will eventually starve the downland flowers of light and warmth. For this reason, sheep are now being brought back in a small way to perform their traditional role and prevent the spread of another kind of habitat altogether.

Rich downland sward at the Castle Hill national nature reserve near Woodingdean.

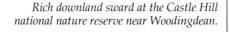

Sheep on the Downs near the Jack and Jill windmills above Clayton. Huge flocks once cropped the turf. allowing the spread of such characteristic sweet-smelling downland herbs as basil, majoram and wild thyme.

21

Common Polypody

Sulphur Tuft

Jew's ear

Hart's Tongue Fern

Stinkhorn

ATLANTIC MEMORIES

*T*o step from warm sunshine into the shady coolness of Fairlight Glen is to journey back eight thousand years through time. Water drips from the leaves of lush ferns, glistens on the mossed faces of sandstone rocks, splashes by your feet on its steep and clattering fall to the sea. This is the tree-hung moistness our ancestors knew when that rising sea made England an island and the climate became gradually (and for two millenia) oceanic, wet, 'Atlantic'.

A glance at plant distribution maps confirms that this feeling of being in another, older world is no romantic fancy. There are, for instance, more than forty mosses and liverworts which are clustered among the rocky woods of Britain's sea-washed western coasts, from Cornwall up to Scotland, and which are found practically nowhere else - nowhere, that is, but in the wooded ghyll valleys and on the damp rock outcrops of the East Sussex sandstone country. The ivy-leaved bellflower and the Cornish moneywort seem similarly out of place, as do the mountain and hay-scented ferns and a range of others (black spleenwort, maidenhair spleenwort and the scarce rustyback fern) which grow in the crevices of walls.

What are they doing here? A single isolated 'foreign' plant might simply be regarded as an interesting freak, but the presence of so many of them demands a theory: botanists believe that these are nothing less than the relics of the original Atlantic flora of lowland Britain which have managed to cling to life here these many thousands of years because of their peculiar micro-climate - damp and cool in summer, sheltered from frosts in winter. These are the great survivors.

You descend Fairlight Glen under a canopy of sessile oaks, beeches and sycamores (though rather fewer than before the great storm of October, 1987), with an underlayer of alder, sallow and birch. Water crickets inhabit the streams here, feeding on the larvae of midges, mayflies and other flying insects. The wateriness flaunts itself in everything that grows: golden saxifrage, stinking iris, pendulous sedge. Dripping Well (off to your left, going down) is the glen's prime site from the botanical point of view, an evergreen grotto where the rockface, never dry, is overhung by creepers and matted with moulds, mildews and mosses.

The ferns mass thickly wherever you turn, and there are many more species than a casual first glance will suggest: hart's tongue and hard shield, lady and scaly male, broad buckler and (growing on bare rock) common polypody fern. The reek of wild garlic will assail your nostrils in the spring months, while the appropriately named stinkhorn is but one of a rather sinister congregation of fungi. Look out for the rubbery red-brown jew's ear on dying elder wood, for the lemon parasols of young sulphur tuft and the dark stumps of dead men's fingers.

And yet these Wealden ravines - and there are some three hundred of them in all - have their colourful, flying wildlife, too: azure and large red damselflies over the water and through the glades; breeding emperor dragonflies (and sometimes swarms of migrant dragonflies from Europe, too); small skipper, meadow brown and speckled wood butterflies; and, among the birds, summer visitors such as whitethroats, willow warblers and spotted flycatchers. The winter feeding stations in Fairlight Glen have attracted five different species of tit.

Evergreen grotto: Dripping Well in Fairlight Glen.

purple emperor

oak apples

gall wasps

grey squirrel

THE SUSSEX WEED

Woodland covered Sussex before early man set to work with axe and fire, and the felling of such useful trees as elm and lime was soon to leave the mighty oak as the unrivalled king of the forest. No flint tool could easily make an impression on one of these giants in its majestic maturity, and until the advent of iron blades the tree's importance lay in its bountiful crop of acorns, which provided a valuable source of food for pigs in the autumn. Later, of course, its timber was to be heavily exploited as the sturdiest of building materials (in medieval times, when Hastings was the headquarters of the Confederation of the Cinque Ports, the Weald was a major supplier to Sussex shipwrights), but the county nevertheless still retains some fine oak woodlands and a great many splendid individual trees in its hedges and open fields. Kipling wrote rather boastfully of this abundance:

> *I will go north about the shaws*
> *And the deep ghylls that breed*
> *Huge oaks and old, the which we hold*
> *No more than Sussex weed.*

In those ghyll valleys he was gazing mainly upon sessile oaks, which prefer the lighter, acid soils of Sussex. The commonest species in the county, thriving on the deep, wet clays of the Weald, is that other native, the English or pedunculate oak. This wide-spreading beauty, its leaves a ginger hue as they open in the spring, a golden brown in late autumn, can grow to a height of 90ft and will live for approaching three hundred years if spared.

A mature oak wood - especially a managed one which allows other species room to develop - is impressively rich in vegetation. Typical 'junior' members of the tree fraternity are ash and field maple, while an under layer of holly, rowan and yew will give shelter to shrubs such as hazel, spindle tree, blackthorn, hawthorn, elder, sallows and willows. Pushing above the many mosses and liverworts at ground level we might expect to see meadowsweet, creeping buttercup, bugle, enchanter's nightshade and a variety of sedges and rushes.

It is the oak's generous support of bird, mammal and insect life, however, which explains its unrivalled place in the natural history of Sussex. An ecologist's preference for native trees over introduced species has nothing to do with national pride and everything to do with the twin processes of evolution and adaptation. The sycamore, for example, is an otherwise splendid addition to the rural scene, but it was brought here as a garden plant during the sixteenth century, and four hundred years is a relatively short span of time for change in the natural world. Our wildlife has been living with the oak for thousands of years more, which accounts for the (staggering) fact that more than three hundred species of insect are totally dependent upon it. Should the oaks disappear, we would lose them all: mercifully, thanks to the millions of acorns each tree produces in its lifetime, natural regeneration seems equal to the appetites of seed and seedling eaters such as birds, rabbits, mice and voles.

Among the teeming hangers-on are those wasps (nearly twenty different species in all) which have persuaded the oak to deform its leaf or bark tissue in order to create protective galls around their larvae. One of the best known is the oak apple gall - at first rosy pink, but afterwards a dull brown, its crust holed like a collander by the emerging, fully-grown wasps. Newcomers do sometimes arrive, having learnt their trade elsewhere, and a recent immigrant to Sussex is the knopper gall wasp, which makes its gall on acorn cups.

Several butterflies and moths are similarly fixated on the oak, the most impressive of them all being the large, magnificent but rarely seen purple emperor butterfly. The adults are on the wing from the middle of July, but they roost high in the canopy at night and spend much of their time hidden from casual view: their Sussex strongholds are the woods of the western weald, but their true numbers are unknown. The emperors feed on the sap which oozes from wounds in the trunk of the tree and on the sugary, processed sap known as honeydew which is excreted on the leaves by aphids. They do come to ground looking for salt, however, sometimes finding it in animal dung, and they lay their eggs on the leaves of sallows.

An oak in spring foliage. A single tree may be home to more than three hundred kinds of insect.

oak woods:

• *Nap Wood, Frant
(Sussex Wildlife Trust)
188: TQ 582330*

• *Flatropers Wood, Beckley
(Sussex Wildlife Trust)
189/199: TQ 861231*

• *Footland Wood, Battle
(Forestry Commission)
199: TQ 763203*

• *Fore Wood, Crowhurst
(RSPB)
199: TQ 753218*

• *Selwyns Wood, Cross-in-Hand (Sussex Wildlife Trust)
199: TQ 552204*

• *Gillham Wood, Cooden
(Sussex Wildlife Trust)
199: TQ 718069*

• *Marline & Park Woods,
Crowhurst
(Sussex Wildlife Trust)
199: TQ 783123*

Mermaid's purse

Shore Crab

Bladderwrack

Oarweed

Tompot Blenny

SUSSEX BY THE SEA

*E*njoy a walk from Seaford to Eastbourne - taking the rolling high road of the Downs or (keeping a sharp eye on the tides) the low and rocky road of the foreshore - and you may readily forget the damage which has been inflicted on the greater part of our coastline. You'll find no trace of the customary bungaloid sprawl here, and the Cuckmere, which meets the sea between Hope Gap and the gleaming white chalk of the Seven Sisters, is the one Sussex river to have its mouth untouched by traffic and trade. Not only is this is one of the longest stretches of undeveloped coastline in the south-east of England, but since 1987 it has been declared a conservation area, giving it protection (albeit voluntary) 2,000 metres out to sea.

Cuckmere Haven is an ideal place to begin an exploration of shore life, although the wonders of the place include things you *can't* see. A secret marine world exists out there beneath the waves: in the deep gullies of an extensive chalk reef, shellfish are boring holes in the soft chalk; fish and crabs pass ceaselessly among sponges and waving anemones; and snails and limpets graze on colourful seaweeds.

Commercial fish such as pollack, bass, red mullet, plaice and sole are among the denizens of this hidden submarine universe, sharing it with breeds not favoured for the pot: five-bearded rockling, ballan wrasse, the greater pipefish and the long-spined sea scorpion. Old shipwrecks - and there are literally hundreds off this coast - are a favoured bolthole for crabs and lobsters.

Extending from the shingle beneath the cliffs to the low water mark some 200 metres away is a so-called 'wave cut platform', the soft chalk at the base of the cliffs having been worn away by the constant action of the waves and their cargo of hard flints. Here, and especially at Hope Gap (which can also be reached via steps from Seaford Head nature reserve), you can find the fossil sea urchins which, known as shepherds' crowns, used to be kept by country folk for good luck.

As we start down the beach, over lichen-covered rocks which the tide seldom reaches, we may come across the flat, white bone of a cuttlefish, the papery remains of the common dogwhelk's egg-mass, perhaps a 'mermaid's purse' - the egg-case of the common skate. Along this topshore, sandhoppers, flies and beetles will be feeding on debris, the unlucky ones themselves providing a meal for orb web spiders which inhabit cracks in the cliff face.

Naturalists divide the area between the high and low tide marks into several distinct regions, but even our inexperienced eyes will notice that green seaweeds predominate higher up, while reds are more common closer to the water. Seaweeds use chloropyll to harness the sun's energy: the greens use red light, which is a poor penetrator of sea water, whereas the reds assimilate light from the deeper-reaching blue end of the spectrum.

The rocks are covered with shells. Limpets, winkles and mussels are common here, and the holes in a good many of the small, tightly-clustered barnacle shells (as many as a hundred thousand in a square metre) are a sign that their predator, the dogwhelk, has been at work. A sudden spout of water will reveal that the filter-feeding common piddock is close by - although we may already have guessed as much from the holes which this remarkable mollusc is able to excavate in chalk by rotating a shell armed with rasp-like cutting edges. On the lower part of the middle shore we will see the familiar spaghetti casts of lugworms on the wet sand.

We clamber towards the sea over gullies scoured in the rock by the endlessly surging sea. This is a hostile environment for most creatures, but there are beetles here which can survive in crevices covered by the waves for eight hours in every twelve. The rock pools left behind by the retreating tide offer wildlife more tranquility, but anything that lives here must be able to cope with considerable swings in temperature (on a hot day the trapped water will warm rapidly, whereas on a cold night it may be much colder than the sea itself), salinity (evaporation will make a pool saltier, but rain will dilute the brine) and oxygen content (the seaweeds release oxygen in daylight but carbon dioxide at night).

Despite these demands we may expect to find small blennies darting among the fronds of serated wrack and the pink tufts of coral weed; a common shore crab, perhaps, or a velvet swimming crab; colonies of limpets and periwinkles; and a large crop of pretty beadlet anemones and the grey sea slugs that feed on them.

Coastal lagoons, their landlocked waters nevertheless influenced by the tide, have a unique ecology - and a particularly fine example can be seen at Widewater, to the west. At Cuckmere Haven a lagoon excavated as recently as 1975 has already become an important area for birds.

• *Seven Sisters Voluntary Marine Conservation Area from martello tower, Seaford 198: TV 485986 to Wish Tower, Eastbourne 199: TV 613982*

• *Seaford Head nature reserve, with access to Hope Gap (ranger: 01323 870250) 199: TV 507978*

• *Widewater lagoon (Lancing parish council) 198: TQ 203043*

Rock pools:

• *east of Brighton Marina 198: TQ 345029*

• *Rottingdean 198: TQ 365022*

• *Peacehaven 198: 405008*

• *Newhaven (west of harbour) 198: TV 440998*

• *Cuckmere Haven 199: TV 520975*

• *Birling Gap (westwards) 199: TV 550961*

The marine conservation area beneath the Seven Sisters extends 2000 metres out to sea. Note the cracks along the clifftop: erosion is at the rate of two to three feet a year.

27

WHERE DR BEECHING SWUNG HIS AXE

Victorian railway engineers must have been regarded as violators of the rural peace by those who resented the clanking, steaming monsters they unleashed upon the Sussex countryside, but many of the iron roads they forged through virgin territory a century and a half ago are today tranquil avenues rich in wildlife. The Ordnance Survey maps are littered with the routes of these lost railways, most of them axed in the 1960s in response to a controversial report by the British Railways chairman, Dr Richard Beeching. Several, their tracks removed, have become officially designated, waymarked routes which can easily be walked in stages.

The old straight track: a short stretch of the Cuckoo Trail at Heathfield.

Railways, like roads and rivers, are convenient thoroughfares for wildlife of all kinds. Years of neglect along these deserted trackbeds may have allowed the plants to spread unchecked, the foxes and badgers to burrow into the banks unmolested by safety-conscious authorities, but this seizing of the main chance is evident even beside the busiest of our working railway lines. The building of bridges and tunnels, the excavation of cuttings and the throwing up of embankments have created a variety of new habitats - wet and dry areas, open and shady ground - which has been gratefully accepted.

The seven-mile Worth Way (originally the Three Bridges to East Grinstead branch line, opened in 1855) is typical in its diversity: more than 270 different plants have been recorded here. The route passes through wooded country and farmland on beds of sandstone and clay where the trees include oak, ash, wild cherry and birch, with an understorey of coppiced hazel. The embankments, on the other hand, contain a good deal of introduced chalk, rammed into place by the railway navvies all those years ago, and - especially along the section between Rowfant and Crawley Down - these have been colonised by shrubs such as dogwood, field maple, wayfaring tree and guelder rose. And can those be buddleias we see? Indeed: these richly-scented, chalk-loving bushes have escaped the confines of their Sussex gardens and now swarm with red admirals and tortoiseshell butterflies during the summer in this unconventional setting.

Seven Sussex miles are a universe in miniature. Alders and sallows dip their feet in the marshy areas along this line (a tributary of the River Medway cuts through it near Rushetts Wood), while the ponds are visited by frogs, toads, newts, dragonflies and the large and distinctive diving beetle. In the spring there are cuckoo flowers and primroses, cowslips and wood anemones. Squirrels feast on hazel nuts; treecreepers nest in the older trees; and kestrels and sparrowhawks hunt mice and voles over the open track.

The railway was extended east to Groombridge in 1866 (a line which was destined to operate for exactly a hundred years), and this section, largely wooded and following the course of the Medway after Forest Row, is now known as the Forest Way. Mosses and the hard, male and broad buckler ferns are a feature of its deep cuttings, herons, moorhens and mallards of its river banks.

Longest of the railway walks in Sussex is the Downs Link, which enters the county from Surrey near Rudgwick and threads through the wooded clays of the Low Weald (all three native woodpeckers are found here) before entering the flood plain of the River Adur, where herons fish the ditches and wintering wildfowl flock to the wet meadows.

Overgrown platform at the former West Grinstead station, west of Cowfold, now on the route of the Downs Link walk. Wildlife has swiftly colonised the many disused railways in the county.

Walks along disused railway tracks:

- *Worth Way (West Sussex County Council) from Three Bridges, Crawley 187: TQ 288369 to East Grinstead 187: TQ 388383*
- *Forest Way (East Sussex County Council) from Herontye Drive, East Grinstead 187: TQ 401378 to Groombridge 188 TQ 520368*
- *Downs Link (West Sussex County Council) from Rudgwick 187: TQ 081345 to Botolphs, near Bramber 198: TQ 193094*
- *Cuckoo Trail (Wealden District Council: 01323 443163) from Newnham Way, off Station Road, Heathfield 199: TQ 583211 to School Lane, Polegate 199: TQ 583052*

other signposted walks:

- *South Downs Way South Harting 197: SU 761193 to Eastbourne 199: TV 598983 or TV 600972*
- *Sussex Border Path from Emsworth 197: SU 753058 to Rye 189: TQ 918205*
- *The Wealdway from north-east of Withyham 188: TQ 513376 to Eastbourne Youth Hostel 199: TV 588990*
- *The Vanguard Way from north of Forest Row 187: TQ 435402 to Seaford 198: TV 482992*

see also:

nature's opportunists 78-79

MANY A SLIP

Fulmar on its nest, with thrift.

There's a stunted forest on the fractured undercliff west of Fairlight Glen. Grizzled oaks and willows, old before their time, hunch like bonsai trees against the stiff, cold winds that sweep in from the Channel. To stand among these sorry cripples in Covehurst Wood is to fear that the ground may suddenly shift and slide beneath your feet: the fossil-rich ancient clays and sandstones are notoriously unstable, winter mud slips carrying them away at the rate of several feet a year. This is where the rocks of the High Weald reach the sea, their surfaces cracked and in places hollowed out as caves.

It is, on a fine day, a wonderful place to visit. Whitethroats, nightingales, chiffchaffs and longtailed tits move among a tangle of hawthorn and dogwood shrub, their branches clutched by the tendrils of narrow-leaved everlasting pea. Stinking iris grows here in profusion, its flowers purple, its berries red in the autumn. Common lizards bask on areas of exposed sand, predatory grey bush crickets conceal themselves in cracks in the rock and great

Fulmar

Cormorant

Stinking Iris

Mining Wasp

The view east along the sandstone cliffs from Covehurst Wood. Hastings Country Park extends over 640 acres, encompassing woodland, grassland, heath and cliff.

crested newts swim in rust-coloured ponds rich in iron. Sheltering in the dark underskirts of dense blackthorn scrub, rare mosses and liverworts spread over large boulders, among them (to the bafflement of naturalists) the moss *Eriopus apiculatus* – a native of Australia, New Zealand and South America which really shouldn't be here at all.

And then look up! The rose-pink flowers of thrift are tufted all over the cliff face, while the moist gullies sprout wild celery, common reed and the tall hemp agrimony with its flat-topped ruby-coloured heads. Herring gulls, cormorants, jackdaws and kestrels regularly roost in these cliffs, but there are newcomers, too: the fulmar, which a hundred years ago came no further south than St Kilda but has been spreading very quickly ever since, is now well established; the peregrine falcon is back as a breeding bird, if only tentatively; and in 1993 a black redstart bred here for the first time.

The characteristic plants and insects of this coastal, sandstone environment can be spotted all along the cliffs between Hastings and Fairlight. At Rock-a-nore, for instance, a little beyond the East Hill cliff railway, thrift, tree mallow, wild carrot, rest harrow and alexanders (its seeds once used in cooking) all grow on rocks close to the footpath, and the grey bush crickets, although quick to hide, are quite numerous. Here, in August, you can watch the fulmars, with their unmistakable stiff wingbeats, following the fishing boats out to sea, where they will remain - far from land, enduring whatever weather winter may throw at them - until they return to their nest sites in late December.

Closer observation is required to watch the mining wasps at work in the sandstone quarry across the road from the entrance to Hastings Country Park. The tell-tale signs are the pock-marks in the rocks, although it almost beggars belief that these can have been caused by a small insect. The wasp *Mellinus arvensis* lays its eggs in a number of separate chambers at the end of the hole, stocking each one with a collection of stunned flies which it has paralysed with its sting: a nutritious meal awaits the larva when it emerges.

A mining bee, *Colletes daviesana,* is another sandstone burrower, secreting an enzyme which dissolves the natural cement that holds the sandstone grains together. The female makes a pollen paste for her larvae-to-be, just having time to create a row of cells before she dies. Life is, however, a constant battle in the animal kingdom. Our pollen-laden female mining bee has to be constantly on the look out for one of the cuckoo bees, which will attempt to lay its own egg in her hole, and for a silvery parasitic fly whose larva will eat both her egg and the pollen. Her success rate, unhappily, is not very good: up to half the cells are parasitised.

Miner bees and wasps have pitted the rocks with nesting holes in a quarry by the entrance to Hastings Country Park.

• *Sandstone cliffs, Hastings Country Park (rangers: 01424 813225) 199: TQ 860118*

• *Covehurst Wood 199: TQ 850103*

see also:

*Ashdown Forest 16-17
ghyll valleys 22-23
chalk cliffs 36-37*

Yellowhammer

Juniper

Carpenter Bee

Wayfaring Tree

DOWNLAND INTERLOPERS

*I*t isn't so very long ago that the mention of downland scrub would almost unfailingly bring a curl to the Sussex naturalist's lip, and for good reason. Between 1966 and 1980 bushy shrubs advanced like a ragged but invincible army across more than a tenth of the county's precious chalk grassland, threatening the rich diversity of flowers which – being mostly southern species – need the warmth and light which only open conditions can give them.

The berries of the wayfaring tree, a common shrub of the chalk, ripen through green and red to black.

Rather more tolerance is shown to these upstart bushes today. If this is partly because their spread has been usefully checked by diligent conservationists, it also reflects an increased awareness that the scrub is itself a distinct habitat which demands preservation. In some areas it is now being coppiced, checking its spread to all-encompassing woodland while at the same time ensuring its survival.

Familiar interlopers in the old sheepwalks are hawthorn (often stunted in growth when exposed to relentless winds near the downland ridge) and wayfaring tree, a viburnum whose berries turn from scarlet to jet black as they ripen. The crimson-stemmed dogwood flourishes on land previously turned by the plough, while gorse spreads rapidly on the more acid soils. Elderberry, blackthorn, buckthorn, whitebeam and wild privet are common members of the scrub thickets, giving protection to spreading bramble bushes at their feet and acting as trellises for climbing honeysuckle, dog rose, sweet briar and - unmistakable in the autumn with its swarms of feathery seedheads - the wild clematis, or traveller's joy.

Scrub undoubtedly lacks the variety of flora and fauna to be found on the old chalk grassland, but it at least offers its compensations. At Harting Down, for instance, the adonis and chalkhill blue butterflies disappeared as the shrub layer developed, but duke of burgundy fritillaries came in, along with carpenter bees which nest - and hibernate - in dead bramble stems. Yellowhammers, linnets, whitethroats, blackcaps and stonechats can be heard singing here during the summer months, while the autumn berries (many of them poisonous to man) attract flocks of birds busily feeding up before taking the long journey south. Winter diners include fieldfares, redwings and ring ouzels.

Juniper, one of our three native conifers (the others being yew and Scots pine) is curious in being found mainly on windswept Scottish mountains and the chalk downlands of south east England. It occurs only locally in Sussex. Two of the best copses can be seen at Harting Down and Amberley Mount, while at Saddlescombe Chalkpit, north of Brighton, the Sussex Wildlife Trust has created a small reserve primarily to protect a colony of junipers - a policy which has led it, ironically enough, to cut back maturing scrub which would otherwise have shaded them out.

Juniper (right) at Saddlescombe, north of Brighton. The shrub is found mainly in two very different environments: the chalk downland of south east England and the windswept mountains of Scotland. Where sheep no longer graze (as at Devil's Dyke, below) scrub quickly invades the downland turf.

juniper scrub:

• *Amberley Mount*
197: TQ 040125
• *Harting Down*
(National Trust)
197: SU 800185
• *Levin Down*
(Sussex Wildlife Trust)
197: SU 888131
• *Saddlescombe Chalkpit*
(Sussex Wildlife Trust)
198: TQ 268122

other chalk scrub:

• *Duncton Chalkpit*
(private)
197: SU 960163
• *Fairmile Bottom*
(Sussex Downs Cons. Board)
197: SU 977090
• *Hollingbury Camp*
198: TQ 324083
• *Ditchling Beacon*
(Sussex Wildlife Trust/
National Trust)
198: TQ 331133
• *Malling Down*
(Sussex Wildlife Trust)
198: TQ 423107

UNINVITED GUESTS

House martins

House mouse

House spider

Cockroach

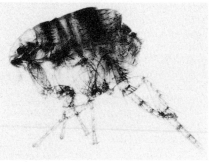

Cat flea.

However welcoming we may be to our friends, however fondly we dote upon our pets, the distinctly uncomfortable fact is that we keep open house to a far greater congregation of crawling, scuttling and flying visitors eager to take advantage of the warmth, food and shelter which our homes provide. Although some are familiar companions (a wide range of spiders, silverfish, house and field mice, bluebottles and other flies in the hot summer months, wasps in August), the mercy is that so many remain hidden from our sight.

Modern hygiene and higher living standards have, it is true, combined to reduce the numbers of some of them. Few of us are now troubled by bed bugs, and the flea that bites us will almost certainly come from a cat: the traditional human variety, which prefers cool, damp buildings, is now rarely seen, or felt, and the last British flea circus which depended on it closed down during the 1970s. Yet the very snugness of the modern centrally-heated home enables insects - some of them tropical in origin - to breed all the year round. The black garden ant is increasingly moving indoors, nesting under floors and in cavity walls. Cockroaches, capable of carrying more than forty diseases, breed copiously in the heating ducts of multi-storey blocks of flats.

Our textiles, unless we buy synthetic fibres only, are constantly chewed by moth and beetle grubs able to digest the keratin of wool, fur, hair and feathers. The brown house moth, a resident of carpets, underfelts and the fluff which collects between floorboards, is a highly adaptable scavenger, with a diet that also includes leather, cork and dried fruit. More common still is the varied carpet beetle, which looks like a tiny mottled brown and cream ladybird and has become the major textile pest in Sussex. The female, having fed on the pollen and nectar of plants such as hogweed and spiraea, flies indoors to lay its eggs: fitted carpets are

The brown house moth, which lives in carpets, underfelts and the fluff that collects between floorboards, is a scavenger with an impressively varied diet.

34

a preferred habitat for the emerging grubs, but abandoned birds' nests in the roof spaces also serve very well.

The very fabric of our buildings may be under attack, too. Oak timbers are prone to infestation by the death-watch beetle (its supposedly fateful ticking sound is a springtime mating call produced by the beating of its head on the wood), but the common furniture beetle is a much more widespread scourge, those familiar woodworm holes being caused by the mature adult gnawing its way to freedom after three years as a slowly-developing grub. And if the insects don't get you, the fungi will: dry and wet rot are the result of minute airborne spores germinating on damp wood in areas of poor ventilation, the strands of fungus feeding on cellulose in the timber.

Some of our doubtful uninvited guests we may enjoy (or *learn* to enjoy) having around. Wasps can certainly become an unacceptable nuisance, but anyone who has recovered one of their beautiful paisley-patterned nests from the loft must be glad they stayed - if only for a time. Few of us would object if house martins were to build their half-cup nests of mud and grass under the eaves, but roosting bats tend to be an acquired taste. With tree-holes increasingly hard to come by, these much-maligned flying mammals find buildings an ideal substitute, and colonies of up to a hundred pipistrelles will sometimes be found hanging under the tiles or soffits , while brown long-eared and serotine bats prefer to inhabit the roof space. Even if they were not protected by law, we should surely wish to keep them for their healthy appetites: a tiny pipistrelle will devour up to three thousand small insects in a night.

Most bees (and wasps) are solitary, and one to look out for around the home is the tawny red mason bee *Osmia rufa*. It collects mud to build its nest in a convenient hole in the wall - and has been known to fill door locks.

see also:

wildlife in towns 56-57
Roger's garden 62-63
nature's opportunists 78-79

Wot – no cheese?! The house mouse, probably introduced to Britain in neolithic times, will happily live in hedgerows and copses, but finds a warm and well-provisioned home much to its liking: it can produce several litters a year, each with five to seven young. The reddish-brown field (or wood) mouse will also set up home in our buildings.

DUKE WILLIAM'S BEACON

*F*or early Venetian sailors it was 'the Devil's Cape' because of the treacherous shallows at its foot. For the Normans it was the 'beau chef', or beautiful headland, and William the Conqueror used its gleaming whiteness as a navigation marker for his invasion of 1066. For us, adapting the French phrase, it is Beachy Head - at 534ft the highest point on the south coast, the easternmost prominence of a spectacular range of chalk cliffs which runs west via the Seven Sisters to Seaford Head and beyond.

Here we find a stunning reminder of the vast reaches of geological time. This chalk, the remains of countless billions of microscopic algae which sank to the ocean bed during the Cretaceous period when most of northern Europe was covered by a warm sub-tropical sea, accumulated at the rate of about a foot every thirty thousand years. This slow build-up lasted for some thirty *million* years, to form layers of white rock a thousand feet thick. From time to time conditions favoured the creation of bands of flint nodules comprised of silica, the source of which geologists still argue about: the use of flint as a building material is a common, and attractive, feature of downland vernacular architecture.

Today the cliffs are in retreat, eroding at a rate of between two and three feet a year. Chalk, a soft limestone, can absorb a certain amount of water, but when mighty shingle-hurling waves break against it at high tide, the air trapped in the rock crevices is alternately compressed and decompressed until the base of the cliff becomes undermined. If the chalk-face above it has been weakened by repeated freezing and thawing during severe winters it will sooner or later crack and tumble - mantling the base of the cliff until the relentless sea breaks it up and carries it away.

This constant crumbling and falling prevents plants from getting a permanent toehold, although the small hare's ear, a rare

Buck's-horn Plantain

Rock Pipit

and very tiny plant, is found nowhere else in Sussex but at Beachy Head: its survival no doubt depends on the fact that it is spared competition from larger growths. Back from the cliff edge the grassland is rich in downland flowers (Beachy Head has several species of orchid, including the nationally rare early spider orchid), but the chalk-face itself is predominantly bare, with only occasional patches of rock samphire, wild wallflower, buckshorn plantain and hoary stock.

For birds it is a very different matter: erosion is of no consequence to them unless the chalk should collapse under a nest, and the sheerness of the cliff is, of course, no deterrent at all so long as a small flat surface can be found somewhere for the laying of eggs. The narrow cliff ledges between Brighton and Eastbourne provide nesting sites for herring gulls, fulmars, kittiwakes, kestrels and (in some years) rock pipits, while stock doves - which, inland, will happily occupy an old rabbit burrow - lay their two white eggs in any convenient cranny.

The most exciting event of the Sussex cliffs in recent years has been the return of the peregrine falcons after many years away. Once upon a time this was their busiest breeding ground anywhere, but the build-up of insecticides in the food chain made their eggs infertile, their numbers declined and they stopped breeding after 1957. Now they are back, to the delight of ornithologists but, without question, to the discomfort of some other species: peregrines, which will seize birds as large as curlews and mallard, regularly prey on two of their cliff-side neighbours, the jackdaw and the feral pigeon.

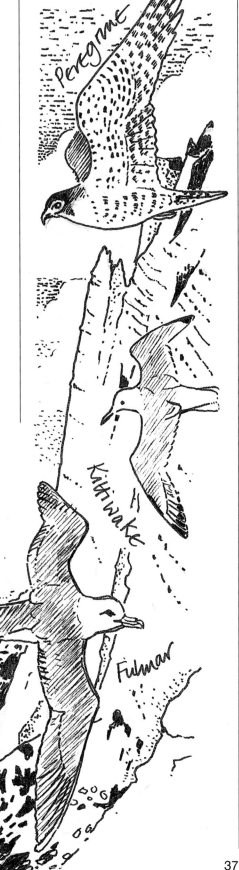

STILL WATERS

A survey of East Sussex ponds during the 1980s found as many as five thousand large enough to feature on the Ordnance Survey 1:25 000 maps. The less pleasing news was that three-quarters of them were in a poor condition, contaminated or choked with silt. Most of our ponds and lakes are artificial: millponds at intervals along every Sussex river; the hammerponds of the Weald, their waters driving the bellows and trip hammers of the great iron industry which thrived here from the sixteenth to the eighteenth centuries; the dewponds of puddled clay and straw on the downland heights, collecting rainwater for huge flocks of sheep. Time and economic change have silently passed them by, and their widespread neglect now threatens, among other wildlife, our dwindling populations of frogs, toads and newts.

Burton Pond, south of Petworth, is one of several which have been preserved. Originally a hammerpond (cast-iron Tudor cannon were manufactured here), it later fed the corn mill which still survives on the site. The open water is a lure for breeding birds such as mute swans and great crested grebes, as well as for a wide range of autumn and winter visitors, while the reedbeds attract the likes of reed

Toads, frogs and newts migrate to their regular breeding grounds each spring and often have to cross busy roads to reach them. Today help is often at hand.

warblers and water rail, but it is the rich aquatic life which concerns us here: a remarkable tally of plants, fish, amphibians, insects and crustaceans. The two ponds at Buchan Country Park, near Crawley, were created for a completely different reason - as ornamental features on a nineteenth century country estate - but they have a similar diversity. Of the 37 species of British dragonflies, darters and damselflies, for instance, as many as twenty have been found here.

A typical large Sussex pond will have, swimming in its depths, such anglers' favourites as perch, tench, the 'foreign' and long-living carp (introduced to England in medieval times; some individuals surviving for more than fifty years) and that aggressive predator, the pike, which will ambush not only sizeable fish but young moorhens, ducklings and water voles. There will be blood-sucking leeches which prey upon fish and frogs, and several kinds of water beetle - including the screech beetle, which squeaks loudly when handled, and the metallic bronze *Donacias* which live under water, their larvae taking oxygen from the tissues of the plants in whose stems and roots they breed.

On or near the surface we shall see water boatmen, pond skaters, fresh-water shrimps, water scorpions and ramshorn snails. We may, in season, see the spawn of both the common frog and the common toad (the former produced as a large mass, the latter in long strings). Both are far more scarce than they once were, but the public awareness of their plight (fostered by the erection of signs in many parts, warning motorists of the routes they regularly take to their spring breeding grounds) has probably prevented an even

One of the two ponds at Buchan Country Park, south-west of Crawley. Twenty species of dragonfly and damselfly have been recorded here.

more serious decline. And we may reasonably hope that all three British species of newt will be present - smooth, palmate and great crested – although the latter increasingly finds garden ponds more to its liking than the often polluted still waters of the countryside.

The native yellow water-lily floats on the surface of our pond, while the plants which fringe it (reeds and rushes, horsetails, loosestrifes, great hairy willowherb) have their own resident insect populations. The county is famous for its rush wainscot moth, which feeds in the rushes of some central Sussex lakes. At Leonardslee Gardens we may see the unusual black and white bee *Macropis europea,* which collects oil rather than nectar from yellow loosestrife and feeds its young a mixture of pollen and oil.

At darkness gathers, the bats emerge. The noctule will be first, sometimes appearing even before sunset to hunt over near-by fields; then, soon afterwards, the serotine, taking moths and chafers in the tree tops; next the tiny pipistrelle, twisting and darting above the water; and finally the so-called 'water bat' itself. This is Daubenton's bat, which flies at a steady 15mph within a few centimetres of the water and will at times take its insect prey directly from the surface, using its large feet as a gaff or its tail membrane as a scoop.

Banded demoiselle.

WOODS MILL

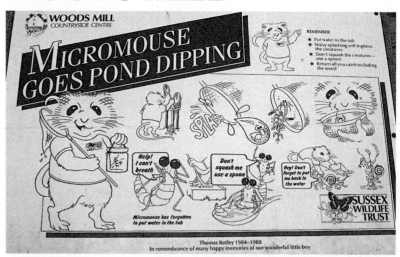

Thomas Botley 1984–1988
In remembrance of many happy memories of our wonderful little boy

he rich diversity of the Sussex landscape is nowhere better demonstrated than at Woods Mill, where 'an ordinary piece of countryside' covering just fifteen acres embraces woodland, streams, pond, lake, marsh, reedbed and meadow. This is the home of the Sussex Wildlife Trust, and an ideal place to begin an exploration of the living world: apart from the reserve itself, with its well-marked nature trail (look out for the bracket fungus on dead birch trees which was once used for stropping razors, and for the teasels used by cloth manufacturers to give their fabric a fluffy appearance), you can enjoy a variety of live exhibits (harvest mice, beetles, fish and, during the season, a teeming bee hive) on the three floors of the 18th century mill house. Here you will find an audio-visual display, a shop and, inevitably, a desk at which you can sign up for Trust membership. In the stairwell, climbing from the bottom of the building to the top, is an oak tree cast in fibre glass, complete with attendant birds, mammals and insects - a striking demonstration of the importance of 'the Sussex weed' to our county's wildlife. In the grounds is a well-equipped classroom which caters not only for parties of visiting school-children but, through one-day or weekend courses, for the curious of all ages.

This little and, at first sight, unremarkable tract of country-side a few miles north-west of Brighton is typical in revealing the resourceful accommodation of birds, beasts and flowers to the many changes brought about by man. There is, after all, a great deal of the 'unnatural' here: the coppiced hazels; the millpond, created by damming one of the two streams (a mill was recorded here in 1374); the large lake, dug out as recently as 1945; and the rectangular pond, originally intended as part of an Italian garden, where visitors are encouraged to trawl with nets for shrimps, snails, water boatmen and the like. The Trust has, in addition, made its own changes since acquiring the land in 1966 - planting an alder copse, developing the reedbed, growing a wildflower bank, creating a new pond.

The reserve may not be known for rarities, but a tally of its recorded wildlife, displayed on a board inside the mill, is impressive nonetheless: plants 263 species; birds 60 breeding species, 37 visitors; mammals 25 species; fish 11 species; butterflies 23 species; dragonflies 14 species.

Greater Spotted Woodpecker

Bracket Fungus

Black & Red Froghopper

Dark-bush Cricket

Moorhen

Birds have taken advantage of every suitable habitat. The graceful grey wagtail, which loves the fast-flowing water of dams and millstreams, and whose presence is an indicator of its purity, can sometimes be seen skimming over the millpond here, its lemon yellow underparts brilliant in the sunshine. Kingfishers breed along one of the streams, reed and sedge warblers by the margins of the lake. The gradual silting up of the lake has deterred the diving ducks and grebes which were once regular visitors, but moorhen are common on the open water, while the reeds and sedges provide winter roosts for reed buntings and the rare cetti's warbler. Woodland residents include tree creepers and both greater and lesser spotted woodpeckers. Kestrels have set up home in a nesting box especially designed to attract them. Tawny owls feed in the wood at night.

Insects are abundant, too. The dark bush cricket and the black-and-red froghopper are found in large numbers, and as many as half the British species of dragon and damselflies have been recorded here. Perhaps the most keenly felt consequence of the great October 1987 storm, which devastated Hoe Wood, was the immediate disappearance of the white admiral butterfly which was adopted as the Trust's logo: it is, mercifully, now back again, and has been joined by brown and white-lettered hairstreaks – newcomers to the Woods Mill list.

• *Woods Mill, Henfield*
(Sussex Wildlife Trust)
(01273) 492630
198: TQ 218138

The lake at Woods Mill, a 15-acre reserve which also includes woodland, streams, meadow, reedbed and marsh.

SAXON BOUNDS

*F*ollow a thick hedgerow along one of our sunken Wealden lanes and you may fondly imagine that it has grown here for centuries past. Count the trees and woody shrub species in a thirty-yard stretch of it (bullace and buckthorn, but not bramble or honeysuckle), and you may well discover that your hunch was right. Historical botanists have a rough, but reliable, rule of thumb based on the rate at which plant seedlings colonise hedges: for each species, they say, you should reckon the passage of a hundred years. Since our Saxon ancestors used hedgebanks as parish and manor boundary markers, and since farmers have, until recent mechanised times, had no reason to grub them out, it should be of little surprise to find that some of our hedges provide a count of ten and more. They have grown here, steadily increasing the variety of their floral habitat and with it a multitude of interrelated insects, birds and mammals, for a thousand years.

The economic value of a well-managed hedge was obvious to earlier generations - for country folk, a regular harvest of fuel, food, fodder and the ingredients for their herbal remedies; for the farmers, a corral and shelter for their stock, a windbreak for their crops, a stabiliser of the soil and a sanctuary for useful insect-eating birds. Changing circumstances have encouraged landowners to create larger fields by grubbing out their hedges, but Sussex is fortunate in having escaped the wholesale destruction suffered by those parts of the country where prairy style agriculture has become the norm.

Many other counties have a preponderance of fast-growing hawthorn ('quickthorn' or 'quickset') hedges which were planted at the time of the eighteenth century enclosure movement - providing, incidentally, perhaps the supreme gift of spring, Shakespeare's darling buds of may. Most of the common land in Sussex, by contrast, had been enclosed long before, which accounts for the grand age and consequent astonishing ecological richness of many of its hedgerows: shrub-counting apart, the presence of field maple, midland hawthorn, hazel or spindle is a useful tell-tale sign of this longevity.

A noticeable feature of the Wealden landscape is its patchwork of irregularly-shaped strips of woodland, known as shaws - remnants (or so their surviving tree types would suggest) of the old wildwood, perhaps spared the axe by medieval farmers

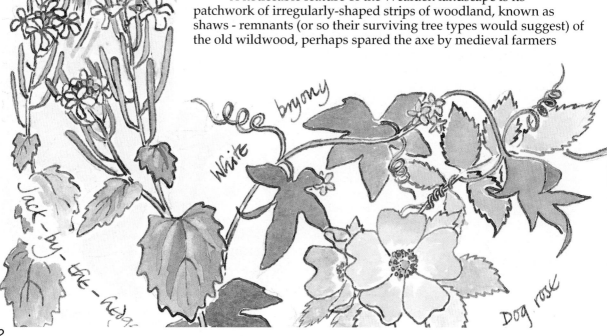

because of the protection they gave against wind and frost. These are, in effect, glorified hedgerows, and they point up the prime value of hedges for the naturalist: the wildlife which thrives here is of the kind which would otherwise be found either in open forest clearings or along the sunlit woodland edges. The hedges, indeed, provide a useful highway along which wildlife can move from one area of woodland to another.

see also:

ancient woodland 10-11
farmland 82-83

And yet, as so often, we have to be aware of habitats within habitats, and here we find, surprisingly, versions of marsh and meadow: the moist depths of the ditch offer an undrained home to marsh-loving plants, while the bank and verge are strips of meadow untouched by fertilisers and herbicides. The elongated nature reserve of the hedge bottom swarms with invertebrates such as ground and rove beetles, centipedes, millipedes and woodlice. Bush crickets start up their evening chirping in late summer and persist until early November. Holly blue butterflies lay their first brood of eggs on holly, a second on ivy. Money-spiders spin the gossamer webs which, drenched with dew, seem to signal the arrival of autumn. Bank and field voles, wood mice, common and pygmy shrews and the appropriately named hedgehog forage among the leaf litter. Rabbits burrow into the banks, which they often share with two of their predators, the fox and the badger.

The first hedgerow flowers of the year are the yellow lambs'-tails of the hazel catkins in February. Next comes the blackthorn, or sloe, its drifts of white blossom emerging before the leaves in March - and its promise of spring so often confounded by the elements that country folk refer to a late burst of chilly weather as a 'blackthorn winter'. At ground level, the lady's smocks, or milkmaids, are among the earliest flowers in damper spots: the very delicacy of their pale lilac petals seems, unjustly, to make them less well known than their companion primroses, violets and celandines. The striking orange-tip butterflies lay their eggs on both lady's smock and another member of the wallflower family, Jack-by-the-hedge - also known as garlic mustard, and traditionally used for making sauces.

Early summer sees the hedges thicken, the dense shrubs sprawling with dog-roses, honeysuckle, white bryony and, in the chalkier areas, sweet-briar and clematis, the verges waving with stands of cow parsley and its umbelliferous relatives. And then the final autumn glory of nuts and berries, of hips and haws, of clambering old man's beard and nectar-rich ivy flowers swarming with wasps and bees.

43

Gorse

Dropwort

Harebell

Bell Heather

Clouded buff moth

CHALK AND CHEESE

An observant walker who follows the South Downs Way west of Eastbourne will emerge from the chestnuts and ash trees of Jevington Holt to discover something decidedly strange about the vegetation. If this is downland - as commonsense proclaims, as the characteristic flora of wild thyme and harebells insists - what are the gorse, the heather and the bell heather doing here? Has some mad plantsman been at work, attempting to overthrow the natural order of things?

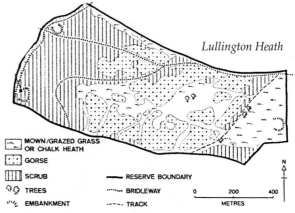

Lullington Heath

MOWN/GRAZED GRASS OR CHALK HEATH
GORSE
SCRUB
TREES
EMBANKMENT
RESERVE BOUNDARY
BRIDLEWAY
TRACK

0   200   400
METRES

N

That the Downs are made of chalk is, like most commonplaces, only a partial truth. Shallow, infertile and calcium-rich 'rendzina' soils may cover most of the range, but there are notable exceptions. In many areas, for instance, the chalk lies under large patches of the reddish coloured 'clay-with-flints', extremely difficult for the farmer to work and, in consequence, often covered by trees: some of the finest Sussex beech woods grow on these soils. In other places the calcium carbonate content has been so thoroughly washed away by rainwater that the leached soil has become neutral, or even slightly acid, encouraging lime-hating plants such as heath bedstraw to move in. And elsewhere there are thick deposits of sandy loess, which geologists believe was blown by the wind from the dry floor of the North Sea during the early part of the last glacial period. These unusual conditions produce the distinctive chalk heath.

Our surprised South Downs walker has, in fact, stumbled upon Lullington Heath, which is managed as a national nature reserve precisely because of this singularity. The sandy soil is nearly neutral but it lies, of course, above chalk. The peculiar result of this is that plants with totally contrasting requirements can be seen growing side by side. Dropwort, a relative of meadowsweet whose clusters of tiny white flowers are somewhat

Two worlds in one. In the peculiar conditions of Lullington Heath, acid lovers such as bell heather and cinquefoil grow side by side with plants of the chalk such as dropwort and a number of grasses, including fescues.

reminiscent of cow parsley, is one downland plant which adapts well to this environment. Another is salad burnet, whose leaves were, indeed, traditionally eaten in salads. The plant has male flowers on the lower part of the head which flower before the female and bisexual flowers higher up - a device often used by wind-pollinated plants to avoid self-fertilisation.

The wildlife of Lullington Heath reflects, as we might expect, the diversity of its vegetation. One of the best areas for enjoying downland butterflies, the reserve also attracts the day-flying, and extremely local, clouded buff moth, an insect of true heathland in other parts of the country.

Chalk heath is rare, but there are small patches of it all along the Downs. You can see it, for instance, at Kingley Vale - on a high point around the memorial stone to Sir Arthur Tansley, the first chairman of the Nature Conservancy (now English Nature) – and in the north-eastern part of the Sussex Wildlife Trust's Levin Down reserve.

• Lullington Heath
(English Nature)
199: TQ 545017

other areas of chalk heath:

• Kingley Vale
(English Nature)
197: SU 826100

• Levin Down
(Sussex Wildlife Trust)
197: SU 888131

• Slindon Estate
(National Trust)
197: SU 960085

• Cissbury Ring
(National Trust)
198: TQ 140080

• Southwick Hill
(National Trust)
198: TQ 236080

• Newtimber Hill
(National Trust)
198: TQ 272121

• Bullock Down
199: TV 578955

A view across Lullington Heath, looking east.

see also:

Ashdown Forest 16-17
chalk grassland 20-21
dry acid heath 76-77

MULTICOLOURED MASTERS OF DISGUISE

Fly orchid

Burnt orchid

Early purple orchid

*F*or their combination of beauty and strangeness, orchids surely have few rivals in the plant world - and, despite the fact that several are threatened by the drainage of bogs and marshes, there are few better places in Britain to enjoy them than Sussex. We had better take our pleasure while we may, however. Since some of the species we find growing in the chalk turf of the South Downs and in the damp woods in the west of the county are at the northernmost tip of their ecological range, they are as vulnerable to climatic change as they are to human disturbance.

A list of Sussex orchids has to be somewhat tentative in view of one of their most striking peculiarities: colonies will sometimes disappear for years on end, seemingly lost for ever, only to spring up again with a conjuror's extravagant flourish when the conditions suit them. At a Sussex site monitored by orchid expert David Lang over a twenty-five period, the numbers of burnt orchids varied from nil in a year of drought to as many as 6,207. Some, moreover, take many years to mature - all of fifteen years in

How was it for you? An early spider orchid being 'mated' by an Adrena *bee which, fooled by the plant's design and coloration, will carry away the pollen on its abdomen.*

the case of burnt orchids. This now-you-see-them, now-you-don't trick offers the naturalist some little hope that rare species not seen here for many years, and then in only very small numbers (slender-lipped helleborine, lesser twayblade, lady orchid) may yet decide that it is time to raise their heads above ground again.

Thinking of orchids in these human terms is rather easy. Charles Darwin, who studied the plants in neighbouring Kent (and who, of course, knew better than to succumb to such anthropomorphic temptations) entitled a famous paper. *The Various Contrivances by which Orchids are Fertilised by Insects.* This apparent cunning is displayed by several of our Sussex species. The fly orchid, scattered throughout the county in light woodland, is so successful in its mimicking of an insect that the male wasp *Argogorytes mystaceus* attempts to mate with its flower, a comical mistake which botanists term pseudocopulation. The early spider orchid uses the same tactic: in this case one of the *Adrena* bees makes amorous advances to the flower, so carrying away the pollen on its abdomen. In the light of these successes it is difficult to understand why the bee orchid, which would seem to rank high among these masters of disguise, rarely attracts sexually aroused insects and has to make do with self-fertilisation.

Below the ground, too, there are artful strategies for survival. In many cases the seeds not only need the correct combination of moisture, oxygen, warmth and light, but they can germinate only if the plant has become infected by a root fungus. Although this initially attacks the orchid, the roles are later reversed, with the plant's cells digesting the fungus - a process which is repeated over and over, the orchid being in the ascendant during its spring and summer growing periods.

The early purple orchid (handsome, but smelling of tom cats) is not only the first to flower but perhaps the best known, since it is very common and grows both on open downland and in chalk and clay woodland. It is soon followed by the early spider orchid on the Downs and the green-winged orchid on clay pastureland, both in flower from late April.

Variations in form and colour are common among orchids. The normally pink-sepalled bee orchids, for instance, are sometimes seen with white sepals and a green lip, while a bizarre form which has been found only in Sussex has the bee-shaped lip replaced by a pink sepal-like structure. There is some evidence, too, that a new subspecies of the burnt orchid is emerging here. This plant, which takes something like sixteen years to flower in undisturbed downland turf, is usually in bloom from the third week in May, but the new form flowers from mid-July until August.

Their weird and wonderful flower designs often give the plants appropriate popular names: lizard and fly orchid, autumn lady's tresses with its suggestion of braided hair. Sussex rarities include the man orchid, a plant of old chalk pastures which is now found at only one downland site: the flower lobes are shaped like the arms and legs of a human figure, the latter sometimes having a small tooth between them.

Another local rarity, until recent years at least, was the lady orchid, which prefers mature woodland on chalk. Although wide-spread in Kent, this beautiful plant was known at a single farmland site in West Sussex - until a heedless herd of cows trampled it to death.

Sussex orchids:

C = common
L = localised
R = rare

(c) coast
(d) downland
(h) heath
(m) marsh
(p) pasture
(w) woodland

white helleborine (w)L
narrow-leaved
    helleborine (w)R
marsh helleborine (m)R
broad-leaved
    helleborine (w)L
violet helleborine (w)L
pendulous-flowered
    helleborine (w)L
autumn lady's tresses (d)C
common twayblade (w)C
bird's nest orchid (w)L
musk orchid (d)C
frog orchid (d) L
fragrant orchid (d)C
greater butterfly orchid(w)L
lesser butterfly orchid (h)R
bee orchid (d)L
early spider orchid (d)L
fly orchid (w)L
lizard orchid (c)R
burnt orchid (d)L
green-winged orchid (p)L
early purple orchid (d,w)C
common spotted orchid
    (d,w)C
heath spotted orchid (h)L
early marsh orchid (m)L
southern marsh orchid (m)L
man orchid (d)R
pyramidal orchid (d)C

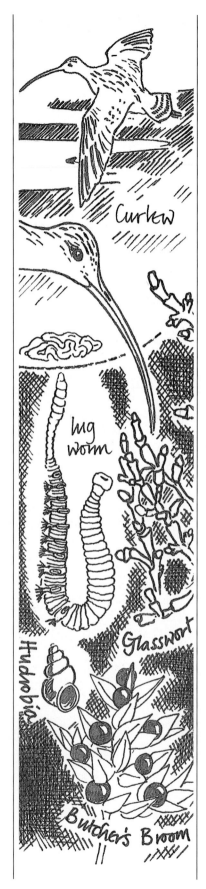

Curlew

lug
worm

Hydrobia

Glasswort

Butcher's Broom

GLORIOUS MUD

Only the hardy visit Pagham Harbour in the depths of winter, when a penetrating wind whips across the glistening mudflats from a cold, grey wash of sea and the shrill piping of an oystercatcher is the sole reminder that there may be any life here at all. These well-wrapped visitors, however, know what they are about - know that when they raise binoculars to their eyes they will discover, in the middle-distance, large flocks of waders and wildfowl probing and sifting for food. Higher up, where long-rooted plants take hold, the sea-washed mud gives way by degrees to dense saltmarsh where geese and wigeon graze.

Since all our Sussex rivermouths have been developed or redirected by man, the county's most extensive saltings are to be found, not around its estuaries, but in the harbours of the far west. At Pagham the entrance was closed in 1876 in an attempt to check an erosion of the cliffs which had already carried away a mill and was threatening the church, but the sea wall was breached in 1910 and several hundred acres of grazing land were reclaimed by the relentless sea. Chichester Harbour has several areas of saltmarsh (at West Itchenor, for instance, and at the south-eastern tip of Thorney Island), but the best lies in Snowhill Creek, behind the protective sand spit of East Head.

If the bare mud appears at first sight nothing but a barren waste, the foraging birds prove otherwise: those hungry waders (oystercatchers and redshank, ringed plover and curlew, dunlin and knot) are excavating for ragworm and lugworm, for small insects, for plentiful snails, shrimps and crabs. As the tide comes in they will retreat to the marshland higher up and to neighbouring farmers' fields. The resident birds share this rich habitat with breeding visitors in the summer and with passing migrants in the spring and autumn months, but the largest influx of all comes late in the year, when huge numbers leave their frozen breeding grounds in the north for the comparative mildness of a West Sussex winter. There have been remarkable bird counts at Chichester Harbour: seven thousand dunlin here at a time; two thousand redshank, 1500 black tailed godwits (a British record) and 1,200 curlew. More than ten thousand dark breasted brent geese spend the winter here - some ten per cent of the world population.

The saltmarsh, with its scant supply of fresh water, is an obvious challenge to flowering plants, and many of them have adapted to it by producing swollen, fleshy stems with no obvious leaves. Seaweeds are so comfortably at home here that more than sixty varieties have been found at the East Head saltings. Green and brown varieties dominate the most seaward of the six zones into which botanists divide this unpromising, yet surprisingly rich, terrain. They not only play an import part in the collection of fertile silt - offering some obstruction to the currents and bringing a little stability to the shifting mud - but they provide a valuable first link in the food chain: sea lettuce, for example, is fed upon by the small snail *Hydrobia*, which is in turn devoured by shelduck.

In the second zone we find the first of the flowering plants - and the only one to spend its whole life submerged by salt water - the misnamed eel grass, which is not really a grass at all. Cord grass, with its stout stems and stiff leaves, is the major plant of the third zone, its extensive root system helping it to form veritable banks of vegetation on the deeper and more mobile muds. A little higher, but still well within the tidal limits where the water ripples towards the sea through sinuous drainage channels, various species of the small cactus-like glasswort become the dominant vegetation: some of them turn a fiery crimson in the autumn. Sea purslane mingles with cord grass in the drier fifth zone, while the higher saltmarsh, which is much less frequently flooded, supports a wide range of plants, among them thrift, sea lavender (a blaze of colour in July and August) and annual sea-blite.

Mature woodland would once have covered the higher ground fringing the upper reaches of the saltmarsh. Oldpark Wood near Bosham is a rare surviving example, with gnarled, lichen-covered oaks lining the shore and, among them, dense clusters of that strange plant butcher's broom, its apparent evergreen leaves being, in fact, flattened stems: according to tradition, the branches were once used by butchers for sweeping their blocks.

• *Pagham Harbour*
(West Sussex County Council)
197: SZ 857965

• *East Head*
(National Trust)
197: SZ 766990

other saltmarsh:

• *Rye Harbour Nature Reserve*
(01797 3862)
189: TQ 941189

• *Pilsea Island*
197: SU 770005

• *Adur estuary*
(RSPB reserve)
198: TQ 211050

• *Ouse estuary*
198: TQ 455002

• *Cuckmere estuary*
199: TV 515977

• *Oldpark Wood, Bosham*
197: SU 823026

The mudflats and saltmarsh of Pagham Harbour attract huge influxes of waders and wildfowl, particularly in the winter months – but binoculars are essential equipment for would-be bird spotters.

Treecreeper

Stag Beetle

Foxglove

Wood Anemone

AFTER THE HURRICANE

*I*n the early hours of October 16, 1987, with barometric pressure plunging to the lowest level ever recorded, the most violent storm for almost three hundred years swept into Sussex - an apparent freak of nature which, for those who experienced its fury, will always be known as 'the hurricane'. Winds of more than a hundred miles an hour shook and battered the county until first light, ripping down power lines, tearing the roofs off houses, making matchwood of sheds and caravans, tossing heavy debris prodigious distances. Five people were killed. If, in the immediate aftermath, the loss of life seemed miraculously low, the damage to the countryside appeared disastrous. Sussex had lost more than five million trees.

Whatever their initial dismay, however, ecologists were soon sounding a remarkably chirpy note. Some fine individual trees were mourned, and the damage inflicted upon small and isolated colonies of plants, insects or bats would take some time to assess, but the overall message was that this ill wind had struck a welcome blow for diversity of habitats. Within three years the Sussex Wildlife Trust was celebrating numerous improvements at Marline and Park Woods, its badly mauled ghyll valley reserve. Species like bluebell and wood anemone had sprung up in the clearings; foxglove, hairy willowherb and red campion were flourishing on newly-disturbed soil; gaps in the tree canopy hummed with sun-loving insects; and grey wagtails, suddenly granted a sight of the stream, were for the first time flitting over the running water. More surprising still, rare mosses and ferns which had seemed doom because direct sunlight kills them had found a new damp microclimate among the tangle of fallen trees across the ghyll.

These were no freak gains and survivals. Nor, as the Trust's Tony Whitbread argued in his report *When the Wind Blew,* was the storm in reality a freak event. Its severity was undeniably exceptional but, since our dominant forest trees can live for up to five hundred years, 'Britain's woods would, in a natural state, always have been in the process of recovering from the last storm.' What our managed woodlands have lacked is the ancient wild-wood's slow cycle of decay and regeneration. We have harvested relatively young timber, lopped dying wood and carted away the dead, so ensuring a uniformity of age among the trees - and, with it, a uniformity of habitat. Commercial forestry obviously demands a large degree of regimentation: after the hurricane it is certain that, outside this category, fewer woods will be as ruthlessly tidied up as before.

What benefits, then, has this stricken timber been seen to bring? Perhaps the most obvious legacy of the great storm's havoc was the light and warmth it let into otherwise shadowy woodland depths, creating conditions not unlike the woodland edges or the newly-cut parts of coppices where butterflies and other insects swarm. Sometimes, when long-buried seeds were brought to the surface, plants emerged which had not been seen on those sites for years. Less obvious, perhaps, were the new microhabitats created when mature trees were toppled by the stormy blast. (If sufficient roots remained in the ground some never-say-die specimens would sprout new shoots from buds below the surface of the bark). A remarkable feature of the post-hurricane landscape was the large number of huge root plates which had been thrust into the air, leaving steep-sided craters in the earth: plants such as reed mace, water starwort and Canadian pondweed quickly colonised the standing water in the base of these pits, while sedges and rushes spread over the damp edges and foxgloves, ferns, mosses and fungi made a home of the root plates themselves.

Decaying wood is itself a valuable, and all too rare, element in the forest's ecological balance. Cracks in damaged trunks make ideal nest sites for spotted fly-catchers and other small birds, while woodpeckers, tree-creepers and nuthatches feast on the ready supplies of wood-boring insects, many of which need a continuity of dead material in order to breed successfully: stag beetles, for instance, have larvae which live in dead wood for upwards of five years before maturing, and some other beetles produce several flightless generations before a dispersing brood arrives. (The elm bark beetle was one of the unwelcome beneficiaries of the great storm). Fungi and bacteria will fasten on to trees which, though badly damaged, may continue to live for many years to come, breaking down the rotting wood and returning its nutrients to the soil.

A last, and lasting, benefit of the hurricane was a growing public awareness. In Bexhill there was so much interest in what had happened to Gillham Wood that the Sussex Wildlife Trust declared it a community wood, with local people assuming responsibility for it: 'What had been a forgotten piece of woodland is now a valued part of the local environment. Because of this, its long-term conservation is more likely.'

• Marline & Park Woods,
Crowhurst
(Sussex Wildlife Trust)
199: TQ 783123

• Gillham Wood,
Cooden
(Sussex Wildlife Trust)
199: TQ 718069

The upturned root plates of trees felled by the 'hurricane' of October, 1987, became new miniature habitats in our woodlands, rapidly colonised by foxgloves, ferns, mosses and fungi. The standing water in the craters they left behind was similarly invaded by moisture-loving plants.

FASHIONED BY WAVE AND WIND

The sand dunes at Camber swarm with holidaymakers during the summer months.

The sea sweeps the sand to the shore, the wind wafts it inland where, lodging against large pebbles or trapped by beach litter and vegetation, it slowly builds into mounds and low ridges. The formation of sand dunes is easy enough to understand: what amazes is the ability of plants to colonise these dry, unstable hummocks against all the odds. This is a landscape always on the move, especially along its seaward reaches. Storms spew up fresh sand and shingle, suck old deposits back down the shore, sculpt deep hollows or 'blow-outs'. As one ridge matures and flattens out, a new one begins to develop in front of it, sifting, windblown sand requiring an initial anchoring by pioneer grasses.

Sand couch grass - a close relative of the gardener's curse, whose spreading rhizomes can tolerate not only salt, but blistering heat by day and severe cold by night - may be one of the first plants to secure a toehold. The coarse, extremely tough marram grass, however, is the great universal stabiliser. At the dunes south-west of Camber village (the only ones in East Sussex), it shares this vital binding role with sea buckthorn, a shrub with narrow grey-green leaves and long spines and which compensates for the low fertility of the sands by storing nitrogen in its roots. The red, white and black-striped caterpillars of the brown-tailed moth (which can cause an irritating rash when handled) spin themselves loosely woven webs among its branches and feed on its leaves. The dunes are dappled with colour during the summer months: the small white flowers of mouse-ear, the orange-yellow of bird's foot trefoil, the fluffy pinkish-white of haresfoot clover.

In West Sussex there are dunes at the Climping local nature reserve, west of Littlehampton, and (though now surrounded by buildings) at Pagham, but the best are to be found at the East Head sand spit, near West Wittering. Here they lie behind a stretch of intertidal sand and shingle. While those closest to the sea are held together principally by the low-growing sand couch, the higher, yellow 'mid dunes' are marram territory - some of it introduced, along with retaining walls of wattle hurdles, after the spit was breached by a storm in 1963. Here, too, there is lyme grass, growing to six feet and with long, numerous rhizomes; the deeply-rooting

Ringed Plover

Marram grass

Sea Holly

Sea Buckthorn

Sea Bindweed

sea holly, a xerophyte with succulent leaves and stems which is able to push through to a new surface when covered with sand; sea spurge, which uses the same head-above-ground survival technique; and sea bindweed, displaying trumpet-shaped flowers similar to those of its country cousin - in this case pink with rose-coloured stripes.

A damp hollow, or 'slack', where marsh flowers grow, separates these yellow dunes from the more thickly overgrown 'hind dunes' - the fixed or grey dunes, their discoloration caused by the humus of decaying vegetation. Patches of bare sand are few and far between now, and there is little disturbance so far back from the sea. The remains of the mosses and lichens which spread here provide a rich source of organic material for flowering plants, the most common being evening primrose, sea spurge, stonecrop, haresfoot clover and hawkweed.

Rabbits are in their element among the dunes, and their holes are sometimes used for shelter by foxes and hedgehogs which raid the nests of ground-nesting birds such as ringed plover, lapwing and skylark. Among insects, look out for the brown leaf-cutting bee *Megachile leachella*, which fashions a cigar-like cell for each egg and can be seen flying with a segment of leaf hanging beneath it. Wonder, too, at the resourcefulness of the sand dart moth: its caterpillar, which feeds on the plants closest to the sea, burrows several feet into the sand during the autumn to avoid being washed away by winter storms.

Sand dunes:

• *Camber*
189: TQ 960186

• *East Head*
(National Trust)
197: SZ 766990

• *Pagham Harbour*
(West Sussex County Council)
197: SZ 857965

• *Climping*
(West Sussex County Council)
197: TQ 015010

see also:

shingle banks 12-13
marine life 26-27
saltmarsh & mudflats 48-49

Sea buckthorn (foreground) and marram grass are the chief stabilisers of the dunes at Camber. The caterpillars of the brown-tailed moth, which spin webs among the buckthorn branches, can cause an irritating rash if handled.

Nightingale

Large-leaved Lime

Sweet Chestnut

Wild Garlic or Ramsons

CUT AND COME AGAIN

Sequestered retreats they may be today, but our Wealden woods were once so threatened by rampant industrial exploitation that a royal commission was set up to investigate their possible obliteration. Although iron ore had been dug out of the ground before the Romans came, the introduction of blast furnaces in the sixteenth century transformed the manufacturing process and made Sussex a major supplier of the Tudor war machine. The arrival of Huguenot immigrants during the same period brought a new impetus to glass-making, which had long been a feature of the sandy western Weald around Kirdford. Both industries did, indeed, consume vast amounts of timber to fuel their furnaces - and yet, whatever the net loss, large areas of woodland survived. The experience offers a corrective to the widespread notion that man's activities are inevitably a bad thing for the environment.

If shipbuilders demanded large oaks to fashion their mighty ocean-going vessels, the ironmasters and glass-blowers found small wood far more useful for their purposes, and they managed their woodlands by coppicing. Our iron age forebears may have been the first to harvest their trees in this way, cutting them back hard so that their severed stumps would throw up strong and straight new growths. By the beginning of the eighteenth century this landscape was covered with coppice-with-standards woodland, the standards being large individual trees (chiefly oak) which were free to spread majestically above the regularly pruned small-fry about them: sweet chestnut, probably first brought here by the Romans; native hazel and hornbeam, the latter a favourite of the Wealden charcoal burners. Chestnut - traditionally cut on a fifteen-year cycle - still remains in some demand commercially, because it splits lengthwise and is ideal for fencing and other garden products.

Coppice woodland is rich in wildlife, but its peculiarity is that the birds and insects have perpetually to 'follow the woodman around'. Within two or three years of a new area, or 'cant', being cleared, the light and warmth which penetrates to ground level produces vivid displays of celandines, violets, wood anemones and primroses, of bluebells, red campion, bugle and wild garlic - attracting a host of butterflies, bees and other insects, many of which are extremely fussy about the plants they like. The caterpillars of fritillaries, for instance, will feed on nothing but violets. The mason bee *Osmia pilicornis* (a bright foxy orange creature which lives in the stumps of coppice trees and seals its cell with chopped-up plant material) has a decided preference for the nectar and pollen of bugle and hairy violet. Nightingales, whitethroats, tree pipits and willow warblers are typical birds of this 'new' territory, giving way to chiff chaff, blackcap and garden warbler as, a few years later, brambles and scrub begin to take over and the trees grow taller and more leafy. Now the pretty ground-carpeting plants, once more suppressed, must await the chainsaw's growl and whine before they can spring up in their glory all over again.

Dormice, today greatly reduced in numbers, require a wide variety of trees and shrubs to feed on, and they do best in mature coppices where, for example, the hazels have grown old enough to produce good crops of nuts. They spend most of their time high in the trees, travelling along horizontal branches, and foresters are now attempting to create the ideal conditions for them - not only putting up nestboxes, but cutting on a longer rotation.

Rich displays of bluebells and wood anemones are a good indication of a really old piece of coppice woodland, since these plants take a long time to colonise. Relics of *former* coppices in the far west of the county include the few, scattered populations of large-leaved lime found growing inside ancient boundary banks along the lower part of the northern scarp face of the Downs: there are about a hundred in a copse at Rook Clift, south of Treyford.

Bluebells (right) at Bates Green Farm, Arlington, for many years a fixture in the calendar for its Bluebell Walk in May. Like wood anemones (below), bluebells are an indicator of old coppice woodland.

coppice woodlands:

• *Idehurst Copse, Kirdford
186/197: TQ 035257*

• *Roman Woods, Rudgwick
187: TQ 110330*

• *Nap Wood, Frant
(Sussex Wildlife Trust)
188: TQ 582330*

• *Flatropers Wood, Beckley
(Sussex Wildlife Trust)
189/199 TQ 861231*

• *Rook Clift, Treyford
197: SU 822183*

• *West Dean Woods (P)
(Sussex Wildlife Trust)
197: 844153*

• *Butcher's Wood, Hassocks
(Woodland Trust)
198: TQ 304150*

• *Wilderness Wood,
Hadlow Down
(01825 509)
199: TQ 534241*

• *Selwyn's Wood,
Cross-in-Hand
(Sussex Wildlife Trust)
199: TQ 552204*

• *Powdermill Wood, Battle
(Sussex Wildlife Trust)
199: TQ 735144*

• *Marline & Park Woods,
Crowhurst
(Sussex Wildlife Trust)
199: TQ 783123*

• *Guestling Wood
(Woodland Trust)
199: TQ 863148*

see also:

*ancient woodland 10-11
oak trees 24-25*

THE URBAN JUNGLE

Feral pigeon

Fox

Built over with bricks and concrete, scoured by traffic, its cosmopolitan atmosphere justifying that old soubriquet of London-by-the-sea, Brighton ought surely to be on the black-list of any self-respecting wildlife. Not so, however - and if its straddling of downland and seashore makes it luckier than most, the town nevertheless stands as an excellent example of what can be found in the urban jungle.

One of Brighton's peculiar advantages lies in the fact that its rapid development as a resort over the past two hundred years (the population was under six thousand in 1794 and still only about 25,000 by 1821) trapped areas of 'species rich' undeveloped chalk grassland within the borough boundaries: the Wild Park at Moulescoomb is perhaps the finest area of relic downland preserved in this way, albeit with some tampering over the years, and as many as nineteen species of butterflies have been recorded there.

The coast has, of course, been overrun with holidaymakers for many generations past, yet here, too, there are surprises. True, the gulls are only to be expected, and the lovely late-April festooning of the cliffs with the fragrant and showy hoary stock may just about be taken for granted since it lies beyond destructive human reach. Shingle banks, on the other hand, are notoriously vulnerable to trampling, and the area immediately west of the marina not only supports plants such as sea kale, sea sandwort, sea rocket and sea bindweed (the latter found elsewhere in Sussex only at Camber and East Head), but has even attracted ringed plovers to nest among its pebbles. There is more life than it at first seems along this ravaged foreshore.

As for the built-up heart of town, the basic attractions for wildlife here are often similar to our own: warmth, security and a good meal. Feral pigeons, descendants of the rock doves bred for food in medieval times, will make a nuisance of themselves wherever kind souls choose to throw them bread and other scraps. Huge flocks of starlings swarm in from the surrounding countryside of an autumn evening, settling like clouds in treetop roosts: the temperatures are higher here, and their predators are far away. Later on, when honest folk are abed, canny foxes will leave their earths in the railway embankment, picking their way along deserted streets to the bins behind restaurants and burger bars.

Like us, too, wildlife prefers to take the shortest cut, and our towns provide numerous 'green corridors' along which animals can forage and plants can spread - a secret network of gardens, parks, street trees and verges, railway embankments, areas of wasteland. Naturalists have identified several of these routes in Brighton, one running from Hollingbury hillfort south along Ditchling Road into the centre, another following the bypass west of Patcham and descending, via Devils Dyke, to the Goldstone area of Hove.

Walls are a habitat which towns possess in plenty, and those in churchyards and cemeteries (undisturbed, and perhaps spared the worst traffic fumes) are often particularly rich in lichens and mosses - for whom the gravestones are an added bonus. The pretty little ivy-leaved toadflax, first introduced to Britain in the seventeenth century, swarms over walls everywhere and is in flower from May until September. The small glow-worm *Phosphaenus hemipterus* (half the size of the more common species, and more often seen in the daytime) has been recorded at

Chelwood Gate, in the churchyard at Buxted Park and on walls in Hastings and Lewes. It preys on snails.

Sewage works produce rich crops of tomatoes, which grow from seeds that have passed intact through the human gut. Rubbish dumps are a fertile hunting ground for botanists who enjoy seeing exotica thriving in Sussex, usually the progeny of garden throw-outs: greater quaking grass, a Mediterranean species grown for flower arranging, is among the more decorative of them. And the generosity of bird and animal lovers can spring surprises on the gardeners in municipal parks: St Ann's Well Gardens in Hove, for instance, often has healthy sproutings of what turn out to be peanut plants, foresighted squirrels having buried some of their tasty snacks for a rainy day.

Alien grasses which sprout from bird seed mixtures (millet, sorghum, stink grass and yard grass) can be seen not only in parks, but in pavement cracks and along road gutters - where many have probably spilled from plastic bin liners. Most are entirely harmless, but there is one occasional escape from these packets which is weeded out by the authorities as soon as it is discovered: cannabis.

see also:

disused railways 28-29
wildlife indoors 34-35
Roger's garden 62-63
Dutch elm disease 68-69
nature's opportunists 78-79

Starlings flocking over the Royal Pavilion in Brighton. Wildlife is drawn to the towns for warmth, security and a ready supply of food.

PAINTED WITH DELIGHT

Mallow

Green
Woodpecker

Cowslip

Bombus
Lapidarius

Older people remember them still - lush, fragrant meadows where bright multitudes of flowers nodded their heads among tall grasses, where butterflies fluttered like carnival bunting and droning bees foraged among the clover all summer long. With may blossom and the cuckoo's song, rustic haymaking in these sun-kissed fields remains a potent symbol of the English rural idyll. Shakespeare wrote of 'daisies pied and violets blue/And lady-smocks all silver-white/And cuckoo-buds of yellow hue' which 'paint the meadows with delight.' Alas, that delight is all but gone. Only a few dozen widely scattered meadows remain in Sussex today, and it is left to our unkempt roadside verges and a few village greens to remind us of the glories we have lost.

Where did they all go? Some were built upon or became golf courses; many were turned to arable; others, while remaining grass-land, became the victims of agricultural 'improvement', their old soil structure wrecked by the plough, the land drained, enriched, re-seeded. Just as the most abundant arrays of downland flowers occur where the soil is poorest, so the variety in a lowland meadow depends upon its being spared the fertilisers which will encourage a few rampant growers at the expense of the rest. Even where meadows were not deliberately treated in this way, they were often given a liberal sprinkling of chemicals carried on the wind from neighbouring fields. Today probably no more than three per cent of the county's original meadowland remains.

Ecologists distinguish between ancient pastures, traditionally sown with plants the animals liked to graze (cocksfoot and rye grass, nitrogen-fixing clover and medick), and hay meadows where the grasses were allowed to grow tall for the season's crop. At this distance of time, however, their lack of disturbance over many years gives the two types of surviving meadow a great deal in common - although old pasture is likely to be littered with large anthills, which often support their own vegetation (mouse-ear hawkweed, heath bedstraw, sheep's sorrel; mosses on their north-facing sides), and which attract that handsome bird with the mad laugh, the predatory green woodpecker.

Grasses such as tall fescue and rough-stalked meadow grass may still predominate in a mature meadow, but many wild flowers will long since have infiltrated themselves, reminding us of Shakespeare's colourful palette: the blues of the speedwells; the yellows of lesser celandine and meadow buttercup; the white and gold of the ox-eye daisy; the reds and whites of the clovers. Voles and wood mice are in their element here, while the vigorous insect

Cowslips are a typical flower of the meadows.

community will include skipper butterflies, day- and night-flying moths and a great many bees, including (although they are much scarcer than they once were) some of the bumble bees: the large red-tailed bumblebee *Bombus lapidarius*, one of the five common Sussex species, sits on her first brood in an old mouse hole, later leaving such humdrum duties to the emerging workers. Swallows, martins and swifts hunt for insects over the meadow by day, noctule bats at night.

Most of our surviving meadows are small and hidden away, but Front Meadow at High Beeches, Handcross (one of several notable High Weald gardens originally created by members of the Loder family) covers all of four acres and is regularly accessible during the season. The underlying soils obviously influence the vegetation, and this is among the finest acid meadows in West Sussex, never having been ploughed within living memory, if at all. The field is mown once a year, in August, after which horses are brought in to poach the ground, treading fallen seed firmly into the soil.

These lucky beasts enjoy a few days' feasting on such a sweet mixture of grasses and flowers that they must think themselves in some equine heaven. Here, in due season, are cowslips and orchids, speedwells and clovers, vetches and buttercups, bugles and trefoils - and a riot of ox-eye daisies.

The flower-rich meadows at High Beeches, which may never have seen the plough.

meadows:

- *High Beeches Gardens, Handcross*
  (01444 400589)
  187: TQ 278307

- *Loder Valley Reserve, Wakehurst Place*
  (NationalTrust 01444 892701)
  187: TQ 338315

- *Winchelsea Pastures, Wickham Manor Farm*
  (National Trust)
  189: TQ 901169

- *Tuff's Hard, Bosham*
  (private)
  197: SU 812013

- *Buxted Park*
  (private)
  198: TQ 488225

- *Marline & Park Woods, Crowhurst*
  (Sussex Wildlife Trust)
  199: TQ 783123

- *St Helen's Wood Meadows, St Leonards*
  (local nature reserve)
  199: TQ 815120

- *Filsham, St Leonards*
  (Sussex Wildlife Trust)
  199: TQ 778098

see also:

farming & conservation
82-83

TRUFFLE COUNTRY

[Sussex Truffle-Hunter, from an original Sketch.]

This woodcut of a Sussex truffle hunter appeared in The Penny Magazine *in 1838.*

Hunters with pigs and sniffer dogs once earned themselves a living in our Sussex woods, tenaciously pursuing a well concealed vegetable prey - a strong-smelling fungus with dark, marbled flesh, which they found down among the subterranean roots of old beech trees. That 'diamond of the kitchen', the truffle, grows there still, if no longer in commercial quantities, one of a special wildlife fraternity especially adapted to life in the cathedral-like gloom of a summer beech wood.

The beech certainly makes life difficult for other growing things. Its shallow roots grow horizontally, starving any would-be rivals of essential water and nutrients. Its dense foliage shuts out four-fifths of the sunlight, catches most of the rain and, when it falls, decomposes only slowly in the shade, with the result that the woodland floor is dry, dark, cool and covered with a thick layer of leaf litter. The specialists of the beech woods are, as we might expect, shade-tolerant devourers of this material: not only aphids, leaf-mining moths and weevils, leaf-hopper bugs and spiders, but leafless plants such as the bird's nest orchid and yellow bird's nest (looking like an orchid, but related to the heathers), both of which obtain their food from the rotting humus. Many species of fungi, those efficient reprocessors of decaying material, likewise thrive in this taxing environment - among them the black, funnel-shaped (and edible) horn-of-plenty.

Where luck and a less intense shade allows, the occasional ambitious young ash will defy the odds, and there may be an under-storey of yew or holly, but the shrub layer is likely to remain poorly developed: some elder, perhaps, and the occasional field maple. At its feet the beech may grudgingly allow the spread of plants such as dog's mercury, wood sanicle, yellow archangel and cuckoo pint. Herbaceous plants, however, had better flower early to stand a chance: columbine, solomon's seal, spurge laurel along the wood's margins. These are granted, it would seem, a grudged existence.

Beech nuts

Beech leaf attacked by leaf-miner

Solomon's Seal

Horn of Plenty

Truffle

But at least this stately tree is generous with its fruit. Those truffle-snuffling pigs were no strangers to the beech woods, farmers having driven their swine to the forests from Saxon times for autumn pannage. The beech-mast is a favourite food of wood mice, grey squirrels (which damage trees by gnawing at the sappy layers beneath the bark) and birds such as jays, rooks and wood pigeons.

While beeches will thrive away from the chalk as long as the soil is sufficiently well-drained, the best of our Sussex woods are to be found along the Downs west of the Arun, many of them covering the steep scarp slopes where oaks find it impossible to compete. Most of them were planted by the great landowners of the late eighteenth and early nineteenth centuries, but soil analysis and the study of mosses and lichens combine to suggest that some of them may be considerably older. The sad fact is that we have far fewer than before the great storm of October, 1987. (The renowned beech forest in Slindon Park Woods was among those wrecked, although there were survivors in Slindon Bottom, to the west of the park). Those shallow roots proved, alas, to be Achilles' heels.

Beech trees at Stanmer Park, Brighton. Many were sacrificed for the Brighton bypass.

see also:

plantation woodland 72-73

ROGER'S GARDEN

*I*t strains credulity, but the experts tell us that the average garden may attract more than forty species of bee and wasp. Such largesse seems a little less far-fetched after a visit to the wildlife haven created by Roger Musselle at Woodingdean on the north-eastern outskirts of Brighton. Here, in a garden 200ft by 40ft, you may hope to spy not only bees and wasps in plenty, but common and great crested newts, frogs and toads; dragonflies; slow worms; banded snails and giant slugs; devil's coach horse, dor and soldier beetles; hoverflies and lacewings; ladybirds and earwigs; house mice and field mice; hedgehogs and, at night, the foxes and badgers which prey on them; pipistrelle and noctule bats; furtive brown rats emerging from their tunnel system under the sheds and compost heaps of neighbouring plots; and a varied and busy fluttering of butterflies and moths. More than seventy-five species of bird have come to the garden since Roger began keeping records of his well-earned bounty, seventeen of them breed regularly and there are some seventy nests here every year.

This is the story of one man's happy obsession. He was just five years old when he arrived here, his family among an army of new settlers whose neat suburban homes were rapidly spreading, avenue by avenue, across virgin downland. In those early days the budding naturalist explored a world he could not know was doomed: a world of fragrant herbs, of voles and shrews, of skylarks, partridges, lapwings, and barn owls, of such an abundance of lizards that he once caught a thousand of them in a single day. Today, in his fifties, he has made some recompense for man's despoiling of the local downland, creating a quite different, miniature habitat of woodland and open glades, of water, rough grasses and nettles.

He is, he will admit, luckier than many. Woodingdean still has its open green spaces, offering routes for travelling wildlife. His lawn is a relic of the ancient turf, with common spotted orchid and autumn lady's tresses, red and white clover, selfheal, plantain and ox-eye daisy. But this suburban nature reserve is essentially the

Roger Musselle's 'top ten' of birds most frequently seen in his Woodingdean garden. The ratings change year by year, with some species particularly vulnerable to hard winters.

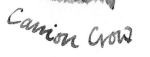

product of planning, patience and a profound understanding of the creatures he loves. Apart from its mixture of trees (oak, ash, field maple, poplar, willows, sycamore, conifers, a sole remaining elm), the garden is planted with berry-producing ivy, firethorn, holly, hawthorn, honeysuckle and snowberry - the latter a particular favourite with blackbirds. Those nettles? Nectar draws butterflies to gardens, but successful breeding depends upon food plants for their caterpillars. Roger has two ponds, one for fish, where toads often spawn; the other totally for wildlife and attracting breeding newts, frogs, water boatmen, pond skaters, water shrimps and water beetles. As winter approaches he puts a bucket upside down in the foliage for hibernating slugs and snails, which are no enemy of *this* gardener: the small white slugs are eaten by the slow worms, snake-like lizards which live in the compost heap, while the huge six-inch long variety take lettuce put out for the pet tortoise. He feeds the birds in winter, makes sure that water is always available.

A bird in the hand. Roger tends a great many sick birds and animals every year: here a young starling seems to be singing for its supper.

Roger's log reveals many changes over the years. Those downland birds may have fled the suburban scene, but newcomers include wood warbler, ring ouzel, greater and lesser spotted woodpecker, long-tailed tit, heron (for obvious reasons), wryneck (twice) and sparrowhawk. The arrival of sparrowhawks may account for the general decline in numbers of tree sparrows and song thrushes - though the latter do well enough in Roger's garden. The blue tit population has fallen severely, but blackcaps and chiffchaffs, once exclusively summer breeding visitors, will now often stay through the winter. This probably reflects a warming of the climate, which would also explain the success of a small colony of grasshoppers (in a small area of lawn left uncut for them) and the arrival from Europe of the brown tree wasp, a large creature with a nasty sting which nests in the firethorn. Losses among the moths include the privet hawk and puss moths (now virtually extinct in the area), but old lady, feather and mother of pearl moths breed in the garden, and the migrant hummingbird hawk moth is a regular visitor. Butterfly numbers have fallen, but Roger's list includes peacock, red admiral, painted lady, tortoiseshell, large and small whites, comma, meadow brown, common blue, orange tip, brimstone, speckled wood, holly blue and skippers.

Among birds the most prolific breeder is the greenfinch, with seven or eight nests each year among the ivy, but these home comforts are abandoned for the security of large flocks out in the countryside for much of the day in winter, and Roger's 'top ten' of most frequently seen species is headed by the starling.

see also:

wildlife indoors 34-35
wildlife in towns 56-57

Bur-reed

Snipe

Fen raft
spider

Frog-bit

Duckweed

BIG SKIES
AND WET FENCES

O n wet winter days the marshes at Pevensey are a
brimming sponge, moist willow country, a dripping
landscape of pools and gurgling runnels under a vast and
often lowering sky. The grassy clumps beneath your feet would be
more yielding still were it not for the complex network of ditches
which, for centuries past, have served both as drainage dykes and
as 'wet fences' to corral the grazing cattle. Now that efficient pump
drainage schemes have sucked the moisture from so many coastal
levels and river flood plains, allowing heavy ploughs to seize the
land for agriculture, ecologists recognise this primitive 'world of
wet' in Sussex as one of the finest in Britain. Along the ditches and
across the sodden pastures you will find as many as 120 rare insect
species and around seventy per cent of the country's aquatic plants.
This is one of only two British sites for our largest spider - the
handsome, and quite harmless, fen raft spider, which can be found
in practically every ditch. Twenty-one species of dragonfly have
been recorded here, and these marshes (like Lewes Brooks to the
west) are an important site for aquatic molluscs. Blood-sucking
leeches live down in the ooze, fastening themselves upon frogs and
fish.

A precious habitat like this needs shrewd stewardship.
English Nature bought 150 acres of undrained fields at Pevensey
Bridge Level in the 1980s and immediately entered into agreements
with neighbouring landowners to prevent further drainage there.
(Although there is no public access, you can get good views of this
national nature reserve from the Pevensey to Norman's Bay road).
Similarly, when the Sussex Wildlife Trust increased its landholding
here to more than three hundred acres, it immediately set about
introducing a network of new sluices in order to keep the pasture
damp in the spring when breeding waders and wildfowl need to be
able to probe for food. Cattle grazing was maintained to preserve
the tussocky grassland in which birds such as snipe and redshank
build their nests - and proved a blessing, coincidentally, for noctule
and serotine bats which feed during the autumn months on the
dung beetles found around cattle. The ditches (most conservations
believe that they should be tick-shaped, with the banks not too
steep) were to be managed according to a seven-year cycle of
clearance and regrowth.

In summer the water channels are dense with vegetation.
When an area is cleared, floating plants such as duckweed will first
move in, followed soon afterwards by the likes of frogbit, bur-reed
and arrowhead along the edges of the brooks and dykes, until
finally there is a choking mass of rushes and reeds. Below the
surface there are newts, toads and frogs - not only the common
frog, but that rampant eastern European interloper with the loud
and echoing cackle, the marsh frog. The playwright Edward Percy
introduced a dozen specimens of this large, mud-brown creature
into his pond at Stone-in-Oxney, Kent, in 1934: within five years the
frogs had colonised 28 square miles of Romney Marsh and were
following the Royal Military Canal into Sussex; by 1952 they had
reached Pett Level (one of the few places in England where the
similarly introduced edible frog can be found); and today, although
their onward march has slowed somewhat, they have reached
Lewes and are still moving westwards.

Most of the amateur naturalists who flock to our wetlands are attracted principally by the large numbers of birds which breed or overwinter there, the former group including the graceful yellow wagtail. Pevensey in the east is matched in the west by the lovely expanse of Amberley Wild Brooks, a few miles north of Arundel (where, below the castle, the Wildfowl and Wetlands Trust has created one of its fine reserves). Because the Wild Brooks have been gradually drying out, however, the neighbouring Waltham Brooks (about a hundred acres; owned by the Sussex Wildlife Trust), and Pulborough Brooks (four times the size; abandoned farmland bought by the Royal Society for the Protection of Birds and now including a visitor centre, wildlife trail and hides) have become important feeding grounds for wildfowl and waders. Controlled flooding and a re-introduction of grazing brought the RSPB stunning results within only two years: ten threatened species had returned to the area in record numbers, while a count revealed that about a half of all the birds in the Arun Valley were to be found at Pulborough Brooks. Wildfowl and waders are the chief beneficiaries of this sympathetic land management, but ornithologists may also hope to see the electric blue of a kingfisher along the ditches and a variety of birds of prey hunting over the brooks - merlins, peregrines and hen harriers, barn and short-eared owls.

The marsh frog, much larger than our native species, has spread rapidly westwards from the Kent border since being introduced in the 1930s. It has a loud, cackling call.

- *Pevensey Levels, north/east of Pevensey*
  199: TQ 650050

including reserves:
- *Pevensey Bridge Level (P) (English Nature) 199: TQ 670057*
- *Pevensey Marshes (P) (Sussex Wildlife Trust) 199: TQ 658058*
- *Hooe Common (Sussex Wildlife Trust) 199: TQ 697105*

other wetlands:
- *Pett Level 189: TQ 900155*
- *Rother Levels 189: TQ 910255*
- *Brede Level 189/199: TQ 860177*
- *Castle Water, Rye Harbour Nature Reserve 189: TQ 941189*
- *East Guldeford Level 189: TQ 950215*
- *Amberley Wildbrooks 197: TQ 030140*
- *Pulborough Brooks, Wiggonholt (RSPB) (01798) 875851 197: TQ 063165*
- *Waltham Brooks (Sussex Wildlife Trust) 197: TQ 025158*
- *Wildfowl & Wetlands Trust, Arundel (01903) 883355 197: TQ 022080*
- *Lewes Brooks 198: TQ 420080*

Pevensey Levels: a world of wet.

see also:

migrating birds 18-19
reedbeds 66-67
rivers 70-71

REED, RUSH AND SEDGE

*C*onsider the humble common reed. Our tallest grass may not be arrayed like the lily, whatever the appeal of those purplish feathery heads, but how it toils and spins! If we in Sussex make scant use of its tough, stiff stems for thatching, our wildlife certainly puts it strenuously to work. The wainscot moths lay their eggs inside those stems, their emerging larvae joining a host of other insects which feed on the plant. The cigar gall fly prefers a developing flower spike for its nursery, checking the growth and creating a deformity which does, indeed, look like a cigar. When the hatched fly emerges the yellow-faced bee *Hylaeus pectoralis* promptly commandeers the chamber for its own nest, often to no avail: in the winter a hungry bearded tit will be along to strip the gall of its succulent grubs.

Reedbeds are generously scattered along our rivers and in our ponds and lakes, with a particularly fine example just above Exceat Bridge on the Cuckmere, but the largest in Sussex lies on the western fringe of St Leonards in the Combe Haven valley. Filsham Reedbed, which covers some 55 acres and encompasses a sedge swamp, open water and drainage dykes, is closed to the public both because of the sogginess of the ground and in order to avoid disturbance to the birds which use it, but a hide along the eastern perimeter gives a good view inside. This was probably once grazing pasture, the plants later spreading out of the ditches to colonise abandoned farmland. Here the tenacious common reed waves in the wind alongside the handsome great reedmace (often mistakenly referred to as the bulrush) with its familiar sausage of female flowers; the bulrush itself, a rush-like perennial with reddish-brown spikelets; and branched bur-reed, which is closely related to sedges and has spherical, spiky flower-heads. Wetland plants such as water violet, frogbit, arrowhead, the tall and pretty flowering rush and the vivid yellow flag grow along the margins of ditches populated by frogs, toads and newts, while dazzling dragonflies hunt overhead.

The common reed is the most notorious clogger of freshwater habitats, its wide-branching root system trapping silt, its new spring growth building on the remains of dead stems so that, uncontrolled, the reedbed will grow higher as well as more dense. The Sussex Wildlife Trust, which manages Filsham, regularly dredges the ditches to prevent choking and cuts each area of reed about once very seven years in order to create temporary open water for wintering birds.

In summer the reedbed is a breeding ground for wetland specialists such as reed and sedge warblers and even on occasions for bearded tits, which a glance at the Sussex bird list shows to be chiefly a winter visitor and passage migrant. By far the busiest times, however, are the migration months when literally thousands of birds drop in to rest and feed. Large numbers of swallows and martins (house and sand) will roost here by night before flying south in the autumn. The little sedge warbler, only five inches long, is a testimony to the astonishing migratory prowess of birds and the richness of invertebrate life in a reedbed: the breeding season over, it will spend several days here, fattening itself on a diet of insects and spiders before flying nonstop to an area south of the Sahara - a journey which takes it two or three days.

• Filsham Reedbed
(Sussex Wildlife Trust)
199: TQ 778098
(reserve closed to public,
but reedbed can be viewed
from footpaths to north and
west, and from hide at the
bottom of Reedswood Road,
off Harley Shute Road,
St Leonards)

• Cuckmere River
199: TQ 512000

THE BATTLE FOR THE ELMS

*T*he first elms began to die in Sussex during the summer of 1971. Their wilting foliage yellowed and fell, leaving branches strangely bare in a green season. If you peeled back the bark you discovered an ugly brown stain over the wood – the sinister fungus *Ophiostomi nuevo-ulmi,* which stealthily choked its victim's water-carrying vessels. Dutch elm disease had arrived with a virulence unknown in living memory, carried here on logs from North America and seemingly unstoppable. Not content with spreading its contagion underground, from root to root, the fungus had recruited large airborne armies of a harmless-looking beetle whose visit now became the kiss of death. Hatched in tunnels under the bark of stricken elms, browsing on the leaves of healthy ones, it ferried the murderous spores from tree to tree. For all that a control area was swiftly created between Eastbourne and Shoreham, where some 80 per cent of the county's English elms were to be found, the trees succumbed in ever greater numbers: more than a thousand infected by 1972; above two thousand by 1974; and a seemingly inexorable increase until, by 1979, the number of new cases was running at well over three thousand a year.

And yet this is a story which promises to have a scarcely credible happy ending, and it begins with that control zone. Easy as it would have been to take a fatalistic attitude to the disease (named, incidentally, after the Dutch scientists who first investigated it), East Sussex county council and the local boroughs decided to fight it. For one thing, they saw a threat to the landscape: elms were the most important tree over a large swathe of land running from the clay soils immediately behind the Downs (where they were a distinctive feature of the hedgerows), along the river valleys of the Ouse and Cuckmere to the coastal towns - Brighton and Eastbourne in particular - where they were an irreplaceable part of the street scene. For another, the local geography seemed to provide them with a defence against new infection: a 'cordon sanitaire' of bare Downs to the south-west, the sea to the south, the emptiness of Pevensey Levels to the east and the predominantly oak woodlands of the Weald to the north.

With legal powers reinforcing a policy of increasing public awareness, the local authorities spent considerable sums of money on felling, pruning and injecting trees until, in October 1993, the county planning officer felt emboldened to make a heady declaration. 'It is likely,' he told the Sussex Downs Conservation Board, 'that the county now contains the only significant population of English elm remaining in the world.'

Some ecologists, taking the longer view, regard this stirring battle as a waste of time and money. Nature, after all, has its own checks and balances and the elms have recovered from apparently disastrous epidemics in the past. Those who seem to have saved the elm for us will counter such lofty reasonableness with the equally incontrovertible fact that our own lives are short, and we had best enjoy our trees and other wildlife while we may - the other wildlife in this case including the attractive, but elusive, white-letter hairstreak butterfly, which lays its eggs on elm (with a distinct preference for the wych elm) and whose larvae feed on various parts of the tree in each stage of their development. They will add that, with the debilitating ash dieback disease threatening the next most important tree in their area, to have washed their hands of the elms would have been to court an ecological disaster.

Has the battle been won? The elm is a vigorous grower which reproduces mainly by throwing up sucker shoots from its roots, and new trees are now sprouting where the old were felled. The critical stage for this 'post-war' generation is when they grow to about fifteen feet and the beetles fly in to feed. While we hold our breath, two new lines of scientific research are being followed. One involves the genetic manipulation of the trees to give them greater disease resistance. The other depends on the fact that the fungus itself has a disease, known as 'd-factor'. If this virus-like agent can be successfully introduced, the elm bark beetle may one day switch sides, burrowing for the tree rather than its destroyer.

Elms are an important part of the urban street scene in the area between Eastbourne (pictured here) and Brighton. English elms, the most widely planted, are more vulnerable to the disease than some other species, such as wych elm.

how the disease is transferred by the Elm Bark beetle

1 dead and dying branches reveal the spread of fungus in tree visited by beetles.

2 fungus, spreading through the tree's conducting vessels, can be seen as a dark band in current year's growth ring.

3 tree gradually dies during the summer.

4 dead or weakened trees provide breeding sites for beetles, which bore maternal and larval galleries in the timber.

5 mature larvae develop, pupate and finally become adult beetles.

6 young beetles emerge: first generation in May/June, second generation in September.

7 fungus-carrying beetles feed on thin bark around twig crotches of healthy trees.

heron

otters

alder

sea trout

TAILS OF THE RIVERBANK

A rustling in the grasses at the water's edge, a brief glimpse of dark, glistening fur, and something far larger than a water vole slips into the rippling current. Which of us has not hoped, at such moments, to enjoy the playful aquatic acrobatics of an otter? Alas for romance and lost innocence: despite reports of isolated sightings, it is several decades since these graceful creatures, the males an impressive four feet from nose to tail, were a regular feature of our Sussex rivers. What we have seen, almost certainly, is a creature half the size - the only alien carnivore in recorded history to have established itself in the wild here, the amphibious North American mink. This escapee from fur farms rapidly colonised Britain's waterways from the late 1950s, first being seen along the Cuckmere and the Ouse in 1964. Two dozen were shot then, and another thirty the following year, but the visitor had come to stay.

The decline of the otter and the rise of the mink are thought to be no more causally connected than the comparably divergent fortunes of the red squirrel and the grey. The mink's success is the easier to understand. Its principal advantage is that it will eat almost anything: fish, frogs and water birds, certainly, but land birds and their eggs, insects and molluscs, rats, voles and mice, rabbits and hares, too. The otter's disappearance, on the other hand, remains something of a mystery, especially as its diet is not markedly different (the sentimental may not care to know that it includes small mammals, ducks and moorhens as well as fish). The activities of the Crowhurst Otterhounds before a self-imposed restriction in 1970 obviously played some part in the process, but the chief suspects must be water pollution and disturbance of habitat. Sussex has no heavy industry, but its rivers are sumps for the chemicals which leach from farmers' fields (sometimes poisoning, sometimes encouraging the growth of oxygen-hungry bacteria and all-smothering algae), their banks increasingly tidied up or cut through by drainage ditches or lined with hopeful umbrella'd fishermen. If these intrusions have led to a sharp decline in the numbers of water voles (the 'water rats' of common parlance), it is surely little wonder that the otters have gone.

And yet, all this acknowledged, there remain stretches of unspoiled 'traditional' river, especially in the higher reaches, where alders dip their feet in the water; where dragonflies skim over the surface; and where kingfishers and grey wagtails nest. Downstream, where mute swans glide, there is evidently no shortage of food for the ubiquitous herons, some of their prey seized while on a journey between two worlds: sea trout which ascend all of our rivers to spawn (with fish ladders helping them to bypass dams and weirs); flounders, spawned offshore but travelling upstream to spend their first two or three years in fresh water; river lampreys, primitive eel-like creatures which, on maturing, spend several years at sea as voracious predators of other fish before returning home to breed.

Water flow and purity are major determinants of a river's fish population, although stocking for anglers distorts the natural balance to some extent. The clean and well oxygenated headwaters of the Western Rother, a fast-flowing little river with some steep gradients, favours brown trout, grayling, minnows, bullheads and brook lampreys, while its lower stretches are the home of chub, dace and gudgeon. Near Pulborough the Rother joins our largest river, the Arun, whose lower summer flows and warmer temperatures make it a more typical coarse fish river - mainly chub and dace in the upper reaches, bottom-feeding bream, roach and carp in the slower-flowing lower stretches until, below Burpham, mullet and bass replace their freshwater cousins.

Of the five main rivers which drain the Sussex Weald, discharging its waters into the English Channel, only the Eastern Rother follows the east-west alignment of the rock outcrops before running down to the sea at Rye. The Arun, Adur, Ouse and Cuckmere all cut through the Downs, and (because their gradients are shallow) are tidal well inland of them. On the chalk itself there are only a few ephemeral streams - although, as the locals are intermittently reminded to their cost, the Winterbourne at Lewes and the Lavant at Chichester can swell prodigiously at times of heavy winter rain.

Sussex has the remnants of three former canals, too: the Wey & Arun Junction Canal, which once connected the coast with the Thames; the Portsmouth & Arundel Canal, which carried the route further to the west, with a spur running from Hunston into Chichester; and, at the other end of the county, the Royal Military Canal, built from Pett to the Kent border as a defence against threatened Napoleonic invasion. Water borne trade and enemy action long forgotten, these waterways now offer wildlife many of the amenities provided by our natural rivers.

The Arun, largest river in Sussex, above the A272.

• *Arun*
187/198 St Leonards Forest
to Littlehampton
197: TQ 028012
• *Adur*
187 Slinfold (W. Adur) &
198 Ditchling Common (E.)
to Shoreham
198: TQ 255045
• *Ouse*
187/198 Slaugham
to Newhaven
198: TQ 002001
• *Cuckmere*
199 Heathfield Park
to Cuckmere Haven
199: TV 515977

other Sussex rivers:

• *Medway*
187 to Kent border
188: TQ 512377
• *Western Rother*
197 Durford (Hants border)
to junction with Arun
197: TQ 035181
• *Waller's Haven*
to Norman's Bay
199: TQ 689057
• *Eastern Rother*
199 Rotherfield
(via map 188)
to Rye Bay
189: TQ 950180
• *Brede*
199 north of Battle
to Royal Military Canal
189: TQ 909176
• *Tillingham*
199 to Eastern Rother, Rye
189 TQ: 925203

• *Chichester Canal*
from Chichester Harbour
197: SU 827011
• *Wey & Arun Canal,*
north of Pallingham Lock
197: TQ 038214
• *Royal Military Canal*
from Cliff End, Pett
199: TQ 889134
to Kent border
189: TQ 941253

otters in captivity at
• *Drusilla's Zoo Park*
(01323) 870234
199: TQ 525049

LIFE IN THE RANKS

Coal Tit

Speckled Wood

Common Centaury

Wood Ant

Parasol mushroom?

The young trees stand to attention in a forestry plantation, regimented rank and file which, like stern guardsmen on duty outside a public building, seem oblivious of the noisy, colourful scene about them. Their tighter formations can, indeed, intimidate the populace (little stirs within a dense block of conifers), but members of the public who accept an open invitation to inspect these commercial parade grounds will find areas surprisingly rich in wildlife. They will also probably discover more deciduous trees than they expected: the Forestry Commission, which owns and leases land across the county, not only manages several mixed plantations, but at Friston Forest it has established a broadleaved forest whose fringing pine trees merely play a nursing role, taking the full force of the strong south-westerly winds off the sea.

Conifer woods themselves are by no means without life, and once the early thinning has taken place the spreading survivors enjoy rather more informality than before. Mature plantations will attract coal tits, goldcrests (the smallest of our regularly breeding birds) and sparrowhawks, while belts of spruce and pine in particular are the favoured feeding ground of crossbills, their distinctive beaks specially adapted to extract seeds from the cones. These birds rarely breed here, but during autumns when cones are in short supply they will erupt in large numbers into southern and western Europe, and a few of those which arrive in Sussex will stay on the following year to nest. Several fungi grow at the feet of conifers, among them the attractive orange and white (but hallucinogenic and poisonous) fly agaric and two members of the boletus family, with their stout stalks and fleshy caps, the yellowish *Boletus variegatus* and the pinkish-brown *Boletus brinno*.

Softwood is generally poor in insect life, but the Scots pine has some specialists attached to it. The pine hawkmoth, rare here before the second world war, is now common and can be seen, albeit well disguised, on the trunks of the trees during the daytime. The wasp *Passaloecus eremita* makes a nest of moss and lichen in a bark beetle's burrow, provisioning the cells with aphids (an eventual tasty meal for its emerging young), before sealing the hole with white pine resin: a ring of tiny white dots is the give-away for the eagle-eyed. Aggressive wood ants, Britain's largest - black and dull orange, and with a powerful bite - construct their remarkable domed nests of pine needles, twigs and other debris on the dry forest floor, foraging out in long trails to gather the material and firing nasty jets of formic acid at any creature (humans included) which gets in the way.

But the most abundant wildlife in a plantation is to be found along the sheltered rides and breaks, where a warming sun shafts through the trees. This is a habitat with similarities to coppice, wood edge and hedgerow. Here, in summer, the ground is studded with the pink of common centaury, the yellow of bird's foot trefoil, the blues of speedwell, bugle and viper's bugloss. Jays and magpies will be busy in the bordering trees, terrifying the smaller birds whose eggs they hope to seize, while pairs of speckled wood butterflies appear to be locked in a frantic dance about your head. Both, in fact, are males, and one is fiercely defending its gradually shifting territory - an energy-giving spot of sunlight.

Light and shade. Plantation rides, as here at Selhurst Park in West Sussex, offer wildlife warmth, light and shelter.

Forestry Commission plantations:

B = mainly broadleaf
C = mainly conifer
M = mixed

- *St Leonards Forest (C)*
  187/198: TQ 208299

- *Sheffield Forest (C)*
  187/198: TQ 420265

- *Wildham Wood (B)*
  197: SU 815135

- *Selhurst Park (B)*
  197: SU 926119

- *Eartham Wood (B)*
  197: SU 945110

- *Houghton Forest (M)*
  197: SU 995110

- *Rewell Wood (C)*
  197: SU 985080

- *Great Wood, Battle (C)*
  199: TQ 770160

- *Footland Wood (M)*
  199: TQ 763203

- *Abbots Wood (M)*
  199: TQ 555072

- *Friston Forest (B)*
  199: TQ 518002

see also:

Kingley Vale 14-15
hedgerows 42-43
coppice woodland 54-55
beech woods 60-61

WITH A LITTLE HELP FROM MY FRIENDS

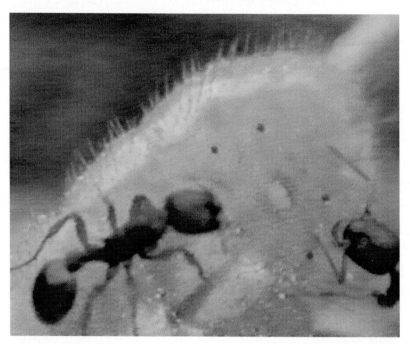

A chalk hill blue caterpillar with its attendant ants.

You'll need the patience of Job to wait for it, and a magnifying glass to make sense of it, but settle down for long enough by a clump of downland vetch and you may witness one of the most remarkable examples of mutual cooperation in the world of nature. Here mingling blue butterflies and ants perform small acts of kindness for utterly selfish reasons, a literal as well as metaphorical back-scratching exercise which rewards one with protection, the other with a sweet potion which drives it close to distraction.

First find your caterpillar, a task for which there is a useful short-cut: the blues are fussy eaters, each species dependent upon a very small range of plants. Now keep a sharp eye on the activities of neighbouring ants. Do they appear to be attacking the poor creature? What they are doing, in fact, is stimulating a porous gland on its back which repays their persistence by discharging a sugary fluid rich in amino acids. The caterpillar's reward comes later in its life cycle as, growing steadily larger, it passes through a series of moults and becomes a chrysalis. Now the ants prepare a safe retreat for it, a hide-away constructed from minute pieces of chalk and other debris close to their food plant. In the case of the silver-studded blue, a heathland species, the emerging butterfly is even given a safe passage to the outside world, where (if it is a female) it will later find a similar plant on which to lay its eggs, starting the process all over again.

Few entomologists, needless to say, have witnessed this fascinating process for themselves, and one man's painstaking labours on a few hundred yards of downland bank south-west of Storrington demonstrate the valuable role which amateur naturalists can play in wildlife research. Reg Hinks soon found an interest turning into an obsession, hour after spare hour spent among the vetches and rock rose, watching and recording. The

Common blue

Small blue

Chalk-hill blue

Adonis blue

years passed. He cut back the invading scrub, tugged out long grasses, scarified the ground to leave bare patches which, rapidly warming under the sun, created an ideal microclimate for ants and butterflies alike. He knew his chalk bank with the intimacy of a lover: which areas were first touched by the morning sun and which saw it last in the evening, how quickly the dew evaporated and how long the soil took to dry after rain. He kept guard on an unusual strain of wild violets and made wary friends with an adder which nested under a clump of wayfaring tree.

This astounding patience produced, at length, astounding video film - a full record of a world beneath our feet which few have ever seen. It also raised questions. If, for instance, the so-called 'honey gland' serves to provide the ants with their intoxicating nourishment, what is the purpose of the 'periscopes' which the camera shows intermittently shooting up on the caterpillars' backs while the ants are at their feast? A definite answer may one day be given. In the meantime Reg Hinks, observing the ants' aggressive behaviour at these moments, hazards the guess that the caterpillars are spraying them with some kind of irritant which rouses them from their drunken reverie and makes them alert and responsible guard-ants once again.

Up periscope! The white gland seen shooting up on the back of this brown argus caterpillar seems to make the ants aggressive – perhaps recalling them to their defensive duties. Despite its name and coloration, the brown argus is a member of the blue butterfly family.

blue butterflies and their food plants:

holly blue
(holly, ivy, buckthorn, dogwood)

small blue
(kidney vetch)

silver-studded blue
(gorse, broom, bird's foot trefoil)

brown argus
(rock rose, stork's bill)

chalk hill blue
(horseshoe vetch)

adonis blue
(horseshoe vetch)

common blue
(bird's foot trefoil, medick, horseshoe vetch)

Home sweet home. The ants build a house of chalk rubble in which the caterpillar retreats until, its various moulting stages over, it forms a chrysalis and emerges as a butterfly. The ant at the top of the picture is about to plug the last gap in this colourful structure.

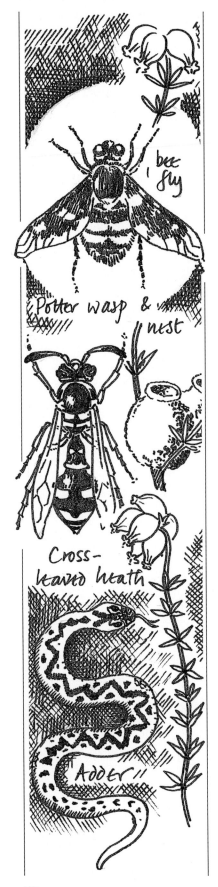

bee fly

Potter wasp & nest

Cross-leaved heath

Adder

THE TEEMING GREENSAND

A tousled panorama of heather and furze, where adders and lizards bask on sun-warmed banks and that acrobatic bird of prey, the hobby, snatches flying insects from the air, the sandy heaths of western Sussex are among the county's best-kept secrets. The narrow belt of lower greensand which runs west from Eastbourne is an inconsiderable feature of the landscape until it approaches the Arun, when it first begins to form undulating hills and then, swinging in a sharp right-hand curve along the Hampshire and Surrey borders, rises impressively to 919ft at Black Down, the highest point in Sussex. It was more than six thousand years ago that farmers first began to clear the oak, hazel and lime from these light soils, which steadily lost their nutrients to a combination of leaching and overgrazing. Abandoned tracts were swiftly colonised by heather, grasses and birch. Today, although they have their scattered wet areas and valley bogs (where sphagnum mosses and sundews grow), the acid heaths and commons of the Midhurst district are predominantly hot and dry. Scots pine, birch and bracken will spread rampantly here unless they are checked, shading out the otherwise thick and wiry matting of ling, bell-heather, cross-leaved heath and yellow tormentil.

This is insect and spider country, a home for species which can survive only in the warm and sheltered conditions provided by the heaths of southern England, and the open sandy areas are especially valuable to them. Here you will find the heath potter wasp, which constructs flask-like nests out of clay pellets and cements them to the branches of heaths and heathers with its saliva. Look carefully and you may see the bumble bee *Bombus jonellus* sitting in an old mouse's nest which it is using for its own. The silver-studded blue butterfly has, like most members of its family, a special relationship with ants, offering a secretion rich in nutrients in return for protection within their nest during the critical pupal stage, and it is not alone in this strategem. *Microdon eggeri,* a little black hoverfly which can be seen flying low over the heather, actually goes one better: ants are reported not only to guard the mollusc-like larvae in their nests, but to groom the newly-emerged adults until they are ready to fly.

But this is red-in-tooth-and-claw country, too. Perhaps the most interesting of the many ants here is *Formica sanguinea*, the slave-making ant, which oppresses one of its near relatives, *Formica fusca:* a *sanguinea* queen will enter a *fusca* nest, kill the resident queen and compel her attendants to raise an occupying army of *sanguinea* workers, while *fusca* pupae taken on a raid may be raised in the *sanguinea* nest, becoming forced labourers alongside their pitiless cousins. The wood tiger beetle, purple-bronze and less than an inch long, derives its name from the ferocity with which it attacks its prey. Two species of sand wasp, each with striking black thorax and red abdomen, hunt caterpillars and take them, paralysed, down their burrows. The bee wolf, a solitary black and yellow wasp which makes a finger-sized D-shaped nesting hole in sandy banks, is the apiarist's curse at the end of a warm summer, catching honey bees and, having paralysed them with a sting, feeding them to its larvae. Other solitary wasps hunt and paralyse spiders, while this teeming insect life itself provides food for a number of heathland birds - hobbies and nightjars, stonechats, linnets and tree pipits.

Like all habitats, this one needs to be managed, especially as some of its wildlife is seriously threatened: the once-common field cricket, for instance, is now found at only one site in Sussex, south of Petworth. Historically the land was extensively grazed, checking the spread not only of tree saplings but of the heather, too. The plant is, of course, beautiful in flower, and many insects rely upon it, but the richness of insect life in the greensand country depends upon the survival of its acidic grassland, too – which means that reserve managers have continuously to cut and clear.

Ambersham Common. Our heaths, no longer grazed by animals or cleared by commoners with rights to small wood and bracken, are quickly colonised by plants and trees which shade out the heather.

dry acid heath:

- *Iping & Stedham Common (part Sussex Wildlife Trust) 197: SU 856218*

- *Ambersham Common (Sussex Wildlife Trust) 197: SU 913194*

- *Lavington Common (National Trust) 197: SU 950190*

- *Coates Common 197: TQ 001175*

- *Wiggonholt Common 197: TQ 060163*

- *Sullington Warren (National Trust) 198: TQ 096144*

see also:

Ashdown Forest 16-17
chalk heath 44-45
butterflies & ants 74-75

NATURE'S OPPORTUNISTS

Magpie

Vetch

Shaggy ink cap

Vole

Uncultivated field edges offer opportunities for resourceful 'weeds' of the farmland.

We can't see them, but they are lying in wait, ever ready to grab their chance. Sooner or later, sometimes much later, the earth will move or the climate will change or the human occupier will pack his bags, and then these stealthy colonisers will seize the territory for themselves - the never-say-die brigade, nature's opportunists.

Orchids are famous for their habit of hiding away for years until conditions are right for them. Leave an ancient lawn uncut for a season, and up they will spring, reminders of an earlier age when this land was theirs by right. They are, however, quite happy to adapt to artificial surroundings: the green-winged orchid (a widespread but decreasing plant of old damp pastures), can be seen in Sussex on the turf roofs of water reservoirs, having smuggled itself in with the soil, while the bee orchid takes kindly to chalkpits and the southern marsh orchid is often found in the rough on golf courses close to the sea.

Herbicides have done for many of the crop weeds which once plagued the farmer, but newly-disturbed field edges will be bright with poppy, field pansy and mayweed, less commonly with the striking pheasant's eye and corn marigold. A few years are as a moment to these resourceful plants with their long-lived seeds.

Ox-eye daisies at South Malling church, near Lewes. Churchyards are often rich in wildlife, their habitats ranging from areas of uncut grass to walls and gravestones.

Many insects, too, enjoy disturbance, especially those which dig in the soil. The bee *Adrena flavipes*, honey bee-sized and with orange legs, is one of several ground-nesting bees and wasps which will make nesting holes in warm, south-facing earth banks: the little 'wasp' which can often be seen in close attendance to it is actually the cuckoo bee *Nomada fucata*, which steals in to lay its own eggs in the holes.

New roads are a gift to enterprising incomers: the early arrivals on an embankment, facing no competition at all, can establish themselves very quickly. When the Brighton bypass cut through the Downs in the late 1980s, dense-flowered and few-flowered fumitory (arable weeds now rare in Sussex) suddenly sprinkled its banks in the Waterhall area where they had not been recorded for half a century: within two years, as sturdier plants grew tall about them, they were gone again. Orchids, as we might expect, are in their element here. Bee and common spotted orchids have become common features of the verges, and the pyramidal orchid in particular thrives on disturbed ground. The edible toadstool known as shaggy ink-cap or lawyer's wig has likewise benefited from the spread of the motor car, while the treating of roads in wintry weather has enabled the salt-loving Danish scurvygrass to spread inland, where it now flourishes far from the sound of the sea.

However warmly these meadow-like strips may be welcomed (and the highway authorities now actively encourage them), botanists nevertheless warn against the indiscriminate strewing of verges and embankments with seed mixes. Some of these introduced seeds come from foreign plants which, though they may be closely related to our own, have undergone no ages-long genetic adaptation to our soils and climate and may have no natural checks from pests and diseases. The danger is that these alien growths will rampage through our countryside to the detriment of its native flowers: we can already witness the rapid spread alongside Sussex roads of the European species of kidney vetch, a bigger and bushier version of our own.

Plants which enjoy undisturbed soil can often be found around the footings of roadside signs. The embankments themselves are not only wild flower havens, but wildlife corridors along which plants and animals can travel.

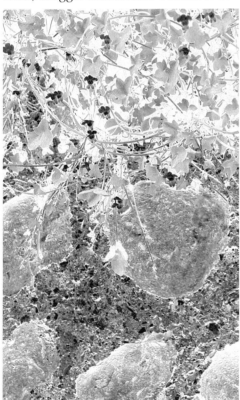

Ivy-leaved toadflax, introduced from the Mediterranean in the seventeenth century, spreads along seemingly inhospitable surfaces – as over the flint of this twitten wall in Lewes. Its pink, snapdragon-like flowers can be seen from May to September.

The first plants are outriders to a wide range of wildlife. Kidney vetch, a coloniser of bare chalk, attracts the small blue butterfly, which has moved in from adjacent grassland to establish strong colonies on several cuttings through the Downs. Essex and small skippers are other familiar butterflies of the grass verges. As the vegetation thickens, so mice and voles forage in the undergrowth and often venture out to be squashed beneath passing cars, making the roadsides a happy hunting ground for scavengers and predators alike. Crows and magpies are eager snappers-up of accidental trifles, while it sometimes seems as if every mile of our major Sussex roads is graced by that eagle-eyed wind-hover, the kestrel.

see also:

MY LORD'S DEER PARK

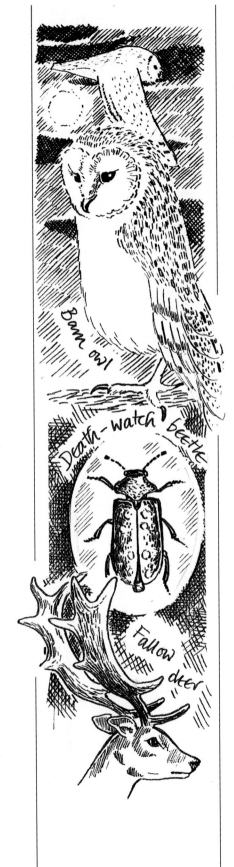

Barn owl

Death-watch beetle

Fallow deer

Parham Park is a fine Elizabethan manor house, with a wonderful long gallery and a great hall in which Good Queen Bess herself is reputed to have dined, but the trees in its grounds have a far older story to tell. For all that the evidence is displayed in glowing colours, however, very few think to look for it, and fewer still have the knowledge to interpret it.

Our first faint clue is the animal grid we cross as we enter the estate; the second is a herd of fallow deer, some two hundred strong; and the third is the grand age of the oaks under which they graze. Approach these trees when the sun is on their trunks and a patchwork of yellows, greys and whites burns with an almost heraldic brilliance. These are lichens, each crust and tuft a mutually beneficial liaison between a fungus and an alga. Just as a count of shrub species indicates the age of a hedgerow, so the lichen profile records a woodland's history - and what these gaudy splashes reveal about Parham is remarkable. Not only was this a deer park long before Henry VIII snatched the estate from the Monastery of Westminster in 1540 and granted it to a wealthy London merchant, but it is almost certainly a rare relic of the prehistoric wildwood which had largely disappeared from southern Britain by Roman times.

Lichens need clean air, light, shelter from drying winds and (because some types take a very long time to establish themselves) a stable

Antler trophies at Parham.

environment. Many of these trees have been standing here for hundreds of years, but what matters even more is the continuity of the woodland of which they form a part. The deer parks of Sussex, producing a valuable supply of winter meat, were often developed on land too poor ever to have been worth farming. In managing their timber as best suited their pockets, moreover, their owners unwittingly recreated the conditions which had existed in these small remnants of the wildwood when they were part of an extensive lowland forest. True, the trees were commonly pollarded to produce a steady head-height supply of small wood beyond the reach of browsing animals, but they were spared the axe because of the shelter and fodder they gave the deer. A similar kind of 'wood pasture' was practised on the woodland commons at Ebernoe and the Mens, where grazing livestock prevented the spread of scrub and brambles in a landscape characterised by a mosaic of open glades among trees of varying ages - from up-and-coming saplings to slowly decaying ancients.

Only Parham and Petworth still have their herds of deer (and the grounds at Petworth were transformed by the landscape gardening of Capability Brown in the 1750s), but ancient, lichen-spattered trees can still be found on the sites of several former deer parks. Dr Francis Rose, constructing a prodigious 'index of ecological continuity' which can be used to establish a wood's venerability, has found huge numbers of lichens at some of them. Parham, the richest of all, has nearly two hundred species (as well as some mosses found nowhere else in Sussex), while Eridge and Ashburnham follow very close behind. Perhaps the most surprising relic of all - since the garden is best known for its exotic trees and Himalayan shrubs - is the area of old oaks at Sheffield Park, to the east of the lake known as Upper Woman's Way.

But old and dying trees offer a home to much more than lichens and mosses. Various kinds of bracket fungus play an important role in timber decay, releasing millions of tiny reproductive spores from tubes along their outer edges. Deathwatch, stag and sawyer beetles lead a vigorous army of wood-boring insects, attracting in turn the birds and mammals which feed on them. Woodpeckers, which drum an echoing tattoo on resonant dead branches, peck themselves holes for nests, while hollow trees are the favourite breeding place of the largest of our three resident owls, the tawny owl.

Fallow deer by the dovecote at Parham. Nearly two hundred species of lichen have been recorded in the deer park, suggesting a continuity of use over hundreds of years.

- *Parham Park*
  (park private, but road to house & garden runs through)
  (01903) 742021
  197: TQ 060143

other medieval deer parks:

- *Eridge Park*
  (private)
  188: TQ 570355

- *Eastdean Park*
  (private)
  197: TQ 900115

- *Pads Wood*
  (private)
  197: SU 785164

- *Petworth Park*
  (National Trust; 01798 42207)
  197: SU 976219

- *Sheffield Park,*
  (National Trust; 01825 790231)
  198: TQ 413242

- *Ashburnham Park*
  (private)
  199: TQ 690146

see also:

ancient woodland 10-11
oak trees 24-25
after the hurricane 50-51
beech woods 60-61

81

GREEN WELLIES

A young lad, taken on a tour of Sussex farmland by the nature writer Gerard Young, gazed upon the long, straight lines of newly-turned furrows and asked, puzzled: 'Why do they do this? Is it to make it look like England?'

Young was himself an exception, but you can read any number of poems and essays celebrating the countryside without coming across so much as a hint that these beauties might be connected with the business of food production. Are these ponds and meadows, woods and pastures, not our God-given heritage? Should we not by some ancient right enjoy the sight of barn owls and natterer's bats quartering the darkening fields; of seagulls spiralling in white clouds behind the autumn plough; of lapwings and partridges flocking in for winter feeding? The fact is that some eighty per cent of our countryside is actively farmed, and the practices which traditionally made our landscape 'look like Sussex' (Wealden hedgerows, sheep runs on the Downs) were driven by economic necessity. It so happened that, although some inconvenient plants and animals were driven out of this carefully managed environment, the scale and variety of the typical farm encouraged a wide range of wildlife. Our problem today is that the efficiency of modern agriculture - heavy machinery, pump drainage, a cocktail of fertilizers and chemicals - threatens to wipe much of it out.

Any attempt to stem this rushing tide has to begin by recognising the simple fact that a farmer's first priority is to produce food. The agricultural community has its representative share of destructively selfish sinners and environmentally sensitive saints, but most of its members are simply out to make a decent

To make it look like England? Furrows on farmland at Kingston, near Lewes: farmers have made the landscape what it is today, and they have a vital role to play in protecting our wildlife.

living: if changes in the use of land endanger our vision of the ideal countryside we had better either come to terms with that harsh reality or make sure that the owners of the land are compensated for their losses.

But, since neglected acres rapidly turning to waste are of no use to anyone, what kind of a working countryside do we want? The Sussex Farming & Wildlife Advisory Group (FWAG), a collection of individual farmers, landowners and conservationists which runs demonstration farms to prove that commercial farming can be integrated with the encouragement of wildlife, has suggested a number of 'golden rules' in its leaflets and pamphlets:

Farmstead. Avoid run-off of slurry, chemicals and silage effluent. Site new buildings carefully and put up nest boxes.

Farm pond. Dredge out accumulated silt and open up the south side. Fence out stock.

Hedges. Trim only a half of the farm's hedges each winter and aim for tall, thick hedges with some trees. Avoid ploughing or spraying into the hedge base.

Streams and ditches. Avoid pollution. Pollard the streamside willows. When maintaining, work from one side only, or clear short sections at a time.

Field margins. Leave at least one metre of natural vegetation between the field boundary and the crop. Avoid the inadvertent use of pesticides and fertilizers (organic or inorganic) off the main cropped area.

Field corners. Plant up awkwardly-shaped field corners with native broadleaved trees and shrubs.

Marsh. Maintain by traditional grazing, but do not plough, drain or use chemicals.

Coppice woodland. Restore a management rotation to give a regular supply of wood and to create a greater variety of wildlife habitats.

Green lane. Maintain hedgerows either side to prevent over-shading.

Hay meadow. Do not plough, plant trees or apply chemicals. Manage by a traditional grazing/haying regime.

Shaws. Begin a replanting programme to replace mature trees when they eventually die. Plant native broadleaved trees.

The good news comes in various guises. The law now prohibits the use of some of the most pernicious chemicals; a relaxing of food production targets has eased the pressure on landowners to plough up ever more marginal land; and farmers themselves have, inevitably, been touched by the spirit of the age. Many of them are now donning green wellies in the figurative as well as the literal sense - perhaps ensuring that future writers will yet sing songs in praise of Sussex.

farms open to the public:

- *Bartley Mill,*
Bells Yew Green
(01892) 890372
188: TQ 631357

- *Great Knelle, Beckley*
(01797) 260250
189/199: TQ 853258

- *Northcommon Farm, Selsey*
(01243) 602725
197: SZ 853944

- *Grittenham Farm,*
near Tillington
(West Sussex county council)
197: SU 942215

- *Heaven Farm,*
Furners Green
(01825) 790266
198: TQ 406264

- *Church Farm, Coombes*
(01273) 452028
198: TQ 192081

- *Washbrooks Farm,*
Hurstpierpoint
(01273) 832201
198: TQ 279163

- *Quarry Farm, Bodiam*
(01580) 830670
199: TQ 782248

- *Horam Manor Farm,*
near Heathfield
(01435) 812597
199: TQ 575173

- *Seven Sisters Sheep Centre*
Birling Farm, East Dean
(01323) 423302
199: TV 558970

DIGGING DEEPER

Reading:

Although several are now out of print, a good sprinkling of useful books on the Sussex landscape and its wildlife can be discovered in our public libraries. Two excellent general guides are Peter Brandon's The Sussex Landscape *(Hodder & Stoughton) and* Sussex: Environment, Landscape and Society, *edited by the geography editorial committee of the University of Sussex (Alan Sutton). A briefer (but nonetheless magisterial) overview of habitats is the introduction by Francis Rose to the* Atlas of Sussex Mosses, Liverworts and Lichens, *published by the Booth Museum. Garth Christian's* Ashdown Forest *(Society of the Friends of Ashdown Forest) and Richard Williamson's book about Kingley Vale,* The Great Yew Forest *(Macmillan) necessarily have a narrower focus, as does* Discovering Hedgerows, *by David Streeter and Rosamond Richardson (BBC), which recounts the history and seasonal changes of one particular hedge in East Sussex.*

E.C.M. Haes' Natural History of Sussex *(Harvester Press) is a layman's guide which manages to cover not only habitats but a wide range of wildlife in some detail. Books of a more specific nature include P.C. Hall's* Sussex Plant Atlas *(Booth Museum), Michael Shrubb's* The Birds of Sussex *(Phillimore) and Colin Pratt's* History of the Butterflies and Moths of Sussex *(Booth Museum). Although it is not a local book, David Lang's* Orchids of Britain *(OUP) is packed with references to Sussex sites. Among more recent publications,* Downland Wildlife *by John F. Burton and John Davis (George Philip) is a beautifully illustrated season-by-season celebration of its subject.*

Organisations:

Whatever your wildlife interest, there is a Sussex group devoted to it. Since few have offices with permanent telephone numbers, the ideal 'clearing house' is The Sussex Wildlife Trust *at Woods Mill. Membership of the Trust is not obligatory for those in search of such information - although it is, of course, highly recommended.* English Nature, *funded by the Government, is the senior conservation body in the county, while our two county councils are also actively involved in preserving wildlife sites.*

Booth Museum of Natural History, Dyke Road, Brighton (01273) 563455

Chichester Harbour Conservancy, Itchenor (01243) 512301

East Sussex County Council, Lewes (01273) 481400

English Nature, The Old Candlemakers, Lewes (01273) 476595

Farming & Wildlife Advisory Group, c/o Plumpton College (01273) 890454

Forestry Commission (South Downs), Farnham, Surrey (01420) 23666

Forestry Commission (Weald), Goudhurst, Kent (01580) 211044

National Trust (East Sussex), Lamberhurst, Kent (01892) 890651

National Trust (West Sussex), Slindon (01243) 65554

RSPB, 8 Church Street, Shoreham, West Sussex (01273) 463642

Sussex Downs Conservation Board, Storrington (01903) 741234

Sussex Wildlife Trust, Henfield, West Sussex (01273) 492630

West Sussex County Council, Chichester (01243) 777100

Woodland Trust, Grantham, Lincolnshire (01476) 74297

GAZETTEER OF SITES

Although you will need seven Ordnance Survey Landranger 1: 50 000 maps for the whole of Sussex (see inside covers), numbers 197-199 include everything except the northern and eastern extremities. The gazetteer lists sites in order of first appearance in the right-hand margins, where the letter (P) signifies that special permission is required to visit a reserve and the organisations mentioned are the managers, rather than necessarily the owners, of the land. Map references sometimes pinpoint an information centre or visitors' car park; sometimes indicate a general area.

Map 186:
Aldershot, Guildford & surrounding area (this covers a small area of north-west Sussex)

Ebernoe Common ..(ancient woodland)	SU 976278	....p11
Kingspark Wood, Plaistow .....(hornets)	SU 990315	....p11
Corner Copse, Ifold.(ancient woodland)	TQ 023305	....p11
Shottermill Ponds.........(hammerponds)	SU 883324	....p39
Idehurst Copse, Kirdford ....(coppice)	TQ 035257	....p55

Map 187:
Dorking, Reigate and CRAWLEY area (also covering HORSHAM and EAST GRINSTEAD)

St Leonards Forest ....(lily beds)	TQ 212308	.... p9
......................................(Hawkins Pond)	TQ 216292	....p39
......................................(Hammer Pond)	TQ 219289	....p39
...........................(plantation woodland)	TQ 208299	..p73
West Hoathly church ....(lichens)	TQ 363326	.... p9
Bear's Wood............(ancient woodland)	TQ 350387	....p11
Nymans, Handcross(ancient woodland)	TQ 265295	....p11
....(rock outcrops)	TQ 268296	....p23
Ashdown Forest..............(visitor centre)	TQ 433324	....p17
....(bog)	TQ 402328	....p17
Weir Wood Reservoir (bird migrations)	TQ 393347	....p19
Ardingly Reservoir.....(bird migrations)	TQ 335288	....p19
Sheepwash Ghyll..............(ghyll valley)	TQ 207298	....p23
Wakehurst Place ....(rock outcrops)	TQ 338315	....p23
Chiddingly Wood, West Hoathly(rocks)	TQ 345320	....p23
Worth Way, from Three Bridges	TQ 288369	....p29
Forest Way, from East Grinstead	TQ 401378	....p29
Downs Link, from Rudgwick	TQ 081345	....p29
Vanguard Way, from Forest Row	TQ 435402	....p29
Leonardslee Gardens...(hammerponds)	TQ 229253	....p39
Buchan Country Park.................(ponds)	TQ 246348	....p39
Roman Woods, Rudgwick ......(coppice)	TQ 110330	....p55
High Beeches Gardens...........(meadow)	TQ 278307	....p59
Loder Valley Reserve ....(meadow)	TQ 338315	....p59
River Arun, north of...............................	TQ 064250	....p71
River Ouse, north of..............................	TQ 371250	....p71
River Medway, west of...........................	TQ 450355	....p71
Sheffield Forest....................(plantation)	TQ 420265	....p73

Map 188:
Maidstone & the Weald of Kent (including CROWBOROUGH, MAYFIELD and the WADHURST/TICEHURST area)

Hartfield church ....(lichens)	TQ 479357	.... p9
Wadhurst church ....(lichens)	TQ 641319	.... p9
Bewl Water Woods (ancient woodland)	TQ 657326	..p11
Old Lodge nature reserve........................	TQ 469306	..p17
Ashdown Forest ....(bog)	TQ 457323	..p17
Bewl Water ....(bird migrations)	TQ 676338	..p19
Nap Wood, Frant ....(ghyll valley)	TQ 582330	....p23
....(oaks)	TQ 582330	....p25
....(coppice)	TQ 582330	....p55
Penn's Rocks...................(rock outcrops)	TQ 520348	....p23
Forest Way, from Groombridge	TQ 520368	....p29
Weald Way, from Withyham..................	TQ 513376	....p29
River Medway, west of...........................	TQ 512377	....p71
Eastern Rother, west of...........................	TQ 850269	....p71
Eridge Park ....(deer park)	TQ 570355	....p81
BartleyMill............................(farm trail)	TQ 631357	....p83

The lake at Woods Mill.

Map 189:
Ashford & Romney marsh area (for RYE and WINCHELSEA)

Dinosaur footprints, off Pett Level.........	TQ 904145	.... p5
Submerged prehistoric forest.................	TQ 905145	.... p5
Rye Harbour nature reserve ....(shingle)	TQ 941189	....p13
......................................(bird migrations)	TQ 941189	....p19
....(saltmarsh)	TQ 941189	....p49
....(wetlands)	TQ 941189	....p65
Castle Water gravel pits...............(birds)	TQ 938176	....p19
Pett Level ....(bird migrations)	TQ 902146	....p19
....(wetlands)	TQ 900155	....p65

Map 197:
CHICHESTER & THE DOWNS *(exends north of MIDHURST and east of ARUNDEL)*

PROTECTING OUR COUNTRYSIDE: WHAT THE INITIALS MEAN

AONB	area of outstanding natural beauty, designated by the Countryside Commission as a guideline to planners. AONBs cover about a third of Sussex.
ESA	environmentally sensitive area, identified by the Ministry of Agriculture, attracting grants for traditional low intensity farming.
LNR	local nature reserve, declared by local authorities.
NNR	national nature reserve, managed by English Nature.
RAMSAR	wetland site of international importance, named after the venue of an international conference in Iran.
SNCI	site of nature conservation importance, locally identified sites recognised by planning authorities.
SPA	special protection area, identified as an important habitat for rare and vulnerable birds under EC Council directive.
SSSI	site of special scientific interest notified by English Nature, the Government's advisory body on nature conservation.

SUSSEX WILDLIFE LISTS

The small boxes are for those readers who like to tick off what they have seen. Species are given in their accepted scientific order rather than alphabetically. A question-mark indicates uncertainty as to whether the species is properly established in the county.

MAMMALS

This list excludes seals, dolphins and porpoises which are often seen off the Sussex coast, and those species (such as ferret, guinea pig and hamster) which occasionally survive in the wild after escaping but are not known to have formed successful breeding colonies. Bats are listed separately.

C = common
D = declining population
G = growing population
L = local distribution
W = widespread, but not in large numbers

- ☐ Red-necked wallaby (L)
- ☐ Hedgehog (C)
- ☐ Mole (C)
- ☐ Common shrew (C)
- ☐ Pygmy shrew (W)
- ☐ Water shrew (L)
- ☐ Rabbit (C)
- ☐ Brown hare (W,D)
- ☐ Grey squirrel (C)
- ☐ Bank vole (C)
- ☐ Field vole (C)
- ☐ Water vole (D)
- ☐ Wood (or Field) mouse (C)
- ☐ Yellow-necked mouse (L)
- ☐ Harvest mouse (W)
- ☐ House mouse (C)
- ☐ Brown rat (C)
- ☐ Dormouse (W)
- ☐ Fox (C)
- ☐ Stoat (C)
- ☐ Weasel (C)
- ☐ North American mink (W,G)
- ☐ Badger (C)
- ☐ Otter?
- ☐ Feral cat (L)
- ☐ Muntjac deer (C,G)
- ☐ Fallow deer (C,G)
- ☐ Sika deer (G)
- ☐ Roe deer (C,G)

BATS

Compiled by Tony Hutson of The Bat Conservation Trust.

M = regular migrant, V = vagrant, and favoured roost sites for the native species are indicated as C (cave), H (house) and T (tree)

- ☐ Whiskered bat (C,H)
- ☐ Brandt's bat (C,H)
- ☐ Natterer's bat (C,H,T)
- ☐ Bechstein's bat (C,T)
- ☐ Daubenton's bat (C,T)
- ☐ Serotine bat (H)
- ☐ Leisler's bat (T,H)
- ☐ Noctule bat (T)
- ☐ Pipistrelle bat (H)
- ☐ Nathusius's pipistrelle (M)
- ☐ Brown long-eared bat (C,H)
- ☐ Grey long-eared bat (C,H)
- ☐ Barbastelle bat (C,H)
- ☐ greater horseshoe bat (C,H)
- ☐ particoloured bat (V)
- ☐ Kuhl's pipistrelle (V)
- ☐ Savi's pipistrelle (V)

BUTTERFLIES

Compiled by Colin Pratt, official county recorder of butterflies and moths. Records should be sent to him at 5 View Road, Peacehaven BN10 8DE

M = annual migrant
m = often supported by small migrations from the continent
R = rare migrant
r = occasional temporary resident

- ☐ Small skipper
- ☐ Essex skipper
- ☐ Silver-spotted skipper
- ☐ Large skipper
- ☐ Dingy skipper
- ☐ Grizzled skipper
- ☐ European swallowtail (R)
- ☐ Wood white
- ☐ Pale clouded yellow (R)
- ☐ Clouded yellow (M)
- ☐ Brimstone
- ☐ Large white (m)
- ☐ Small white (m)
- ☐ Green-veined white
- ☐ Bath white (R)
- ☐ Orange tip
- ☐ Green hairstreak
- ☐ Brown hairstreak
- ☐ Purple hairstreak
- ☐ White-letter hairstreak
- ☐ Small copper
- ☐ Long-tailed blue (R)
- ☐ Small blue
- ☐ Short-tailed blue (R)
- ☐ Silver-studded blue
- ☐ Brown argus
- ☐ Common blue
- ☐ Chalkhill blue
- ☐ Adonis blue
- ☐ Holly blue
- ☐ Duke of Burgundy fritillary
- ☐ White admiral
- ☐ Purple emperor
- ☐ Red admiral (M)(r)
- ☐ Painted lady (M)
- ☐ Small tortoiseshell (m)
- ☐ Large tortoiseshell
- ☐ Camberwell beauty (R)
- ☐ Peacock
- ☐ Comma
- ☐ Small pearl-bordered fritillary
- ☐ Pearl-bordered fritillary
- ☐ Queen of Spain fritillary (R)
- ☐ High brown fritillary
- ☐ Dark green fritillary
- ☐ Silver-washed fritillary
- ☐ Marsh fritillary
- ☐ Speckled wood
- ☐ Wall brown
- ☐ Marbled white
- ☐ Grayling
- ☐ Hedge brown
- ☐ Meadow brown
- ☐ Small heath
- ☐ Ringlet
- ☐ Monarch (R)

BIRDS

Adapted from the Sussex Ornithological Society's list, compiled by Richard Fairbank, but excluding rarities. The full Sussex List of birds seen in the county numbered 373 species at the end of 1991.

R = regular breeding resident
r = non-breeding resident
B = regular breeding summer visitor
b = visitor which breeds most years
P = regular passage migrant
PA = regular autumn passage migrant
PS = regular spring passage migrant
W = regular winter visitor

- ☐ Red-throated Diver   W/P
- ☐ Black-throated Diver   P/W
- ☐ Great Northern Diver   W/P
- ☐ Little Grebe   W/B
- ☐ Great Crested Grebe   W/B
- ☐ Red-necked Grebe   W
- ☐ Slavonian Grebe   W/P
- ☐ Black-necked Grebe   W/P
- ☐ Fulmar   B/P/R
- ☐ Sooty Shearwater   PA

Species	Status		Species	Status		Species	Status
❏ Manx Shearwater	P		❏ Woodcock	R/W		❏ Grey Wagtail	R/W/P
❏ Gannet	P/W		❏ Black-tailed Godwit	W/P		❏ Pied Wagtail	R/P/W
❏ Cormorant	W/P/B		❏ Bar-tailed Godwit	W/PS		❏ Wren	R/P/W
❏ Shag	W/P		❏ Whimbrel	P		❏ Dunnock	R/P
❏ Grey Heron	R		❏ Curlew	W/P/b		❏ Robin	R/P/W
❏ Mute Swan	R		❏ Spotted Redshank	P		❏ Nightingale	B/P
❏ Bewick's Swan	W		❏ Redshank	W/P/B		❏ Black Redstart	W/P/b
❏ White-fronted Goose	W		❏ Greenshank	P		❏ Restart	P/B
❏ Greylag Goose	R		❏ Green Sandpiper	P		❏ Whinchat	P
❏ Canada Goose	R		❏ Wood Sandpiper	PA		❏ Stonechat	P/B/W
❏ Brent Goose	W/PS		❏ Common Sandpiper	P		❏ Wheatear	P/B
❏ Shelduck	R/W		❏ Turnstone	W/P		❏ Ring Ouzel	P
❏ Mandarin	R		❏ Grey Phalarope	PA		❏ Blackbird	R/P/W
❏ Wigeon	W/P		❏ Pomarine Skua	PS		❏ Fieldfare	W/P
❏ Gadwall	W/P		❏ Arctic Skua	P		❏ Song Thrush	R/W/P
❏ Teal	W/P/B		❏ Great Skua	P		❏ Redwing	W/P
❏ Mallard	R/W		❏ Mediterranean Gull	W/P		❏ Mistle Thrush	R/W/P
❏ Pintail	W/P		❏ Little Gull	P		❏ Grasshopper Warbler	B/P
❏ Garganey	P/b		❏ Black-headed Gull	R/W/P		❏ Sedge Warbler	B/P
❏ Shoveler	W/P/B		❏ Common Gull	W/P		❏ Reed Warbler	B/P
❏ Pochard	W/P/B		❏ Lesser Black-backed Gull	P/B		❏ Dartford Warbler	b
❏ Tufted Duck	W/R		❏ Herring Gull	R/W		❏ Lesser Whitethroat	B/P
❏ Scaup	W		❏ Glaucous Gull	W/P		❏ Whitethroat	B/P
❏ Eider	W/P		❏ Great Black-backed Gull	r/P		❏ Garden Warbler	B/P
❏ Long-tailed Duck	W		❏ Kittiwake	P/W/B		❏ Blackcap	B/P
❏ Common Scoter	PS/W		❏ Sandwich Tern	P/b		❏ Wood Warbler	B/P
❏ Velvet Scoter	PS/W		❏ Roseate Tern	P		❏ Chiffchaff	B/P
❏ Goldeneye	W/P		❏ Common Tern	P/B		❏ Willow Warbler	B/P
❏ Smew	W		❏ Arctic Tern	P		❏ Goldcrest	R/P
❏ Red-breasted Merganser	W/P		❏ Little Tern	P/B		❏ Firecrest	P/W
❏ Goosander	W		❏ Black Tern	P		❏ Spotted Flycatcher	B/P
❏ Ruddy Duck	W/B		❏ Guillemot	W/P		❏ Pied Flycatcher	P
❏ Marsh Harrier	P		❏ Razorbill	W/P		❏ Bearded Tit	W/P
❏ Hen Harrier	W		❏ feral Rock Dove	R		❏ Long-tailed Tit	R
❏ Sparrowhawk	R		❏ Stock Dove	R		❏ Marsh Tit	R
❏ Buzzard	W		❏ Woodpigeon	R/P/W		❏ Willow Tit	R
❏ Osprey	P		❏ Collared Dove	R		❏ Coal Tit	R
❏ Kestrel	R		❏ Turtle Dove	B/P		❏ Blue Tit	R
❏ Merlin	W/P		❏ Ring-necked Parakeet	R		❏ Great Tit	R
❏ Hobby	B/P		❏ Cuckoo	B/P		❏ Nuthatch	R
❏ Peregrine	W/P/b		❏ Barn Owl	R		❏ Treecreeper	R
❏ Red-legged Partridge	R		❏ Little Owl	R		❏ Red-backed Shrike	PA
❏ Grey Partridge	R		❏ Tawny Owl	R		❏ Jay	R
❏ Pheasant	R		❏ Long-eared Owl	W/P/b		❏ Magpie	R
❏ Golden Pheasant	R		❏ Short-eared Owl	W/P		❏ Jackdaw	R
❏ Water Rail	W/b		❏ Nightjar	B		❏ Rook	R
❏ Moorhen	R		❏ Swift	B/P		❏ Carrion Crow	R
❏ Coot	R/W		❏ Kingfisher	R/W		❏ Starling	R/W/P
❏ Oystercatcher	W/P/b		❏ Hoopoe	PS		❏ House Sparrow	R
❏ Avocet	P		❏ Wryneck	PA		❏ Tree Sparrow	W/P/B
❏ Little-Ringed Plover	P/B		❏ Green Woodpecker	R		❏ Chaffinch	R/W/P
❏ Ringed Plover	W/P/B		❏ Great Spotted Woodpecker	R		❏ Brambling	W/P
❏ Golden Plover	W		❏ Lesser Spotted Woodpecker	R		❏ Greenfinch	R/P/W
❏ Grey Plover	W/P		❏ Woodlark	b		❏ Goldfinch	B/P/W
❏ Lapwing	W/P/R		❏ Skylark	R/W/P		❏ Siskin	W/P
❏ Knot	W/P		❏ Sand Martin	P/B		❏ Linnet	R/P/W
❏ Sanderling	W/P		❏ Swallow	B/P		❏ Twite	W
❏ Little Stint	PA		❏ House Martin	B/P		❏ Redpoll	W/P/B
❏ Curlew Sandpiper	PA		❏ Tawny Pipit	PA		❏ Common Crossbill	W/P
❏ Purple Sandpiper	W		❏ Tree Pipit	P/B		❏ Bullfinch	R/W
❏ Dunlin	W/P		❏ Meadow Pipit	R/W/P		❏ Hawfinch	R
❏ Ruff	W/P		❏ Rock Pipit	R/W/P		❏ Snow Bunting	W
❏ Jack Snipe	W		❏ Water Pipit	W/PS		❏ Yellowhammer	R
❏ Snipe	R/W/P		❏ Yellow Wagtail	P/B		❏ Reed Bunting	R/P/W
						❏ Corn Bunting	R

INDEX